Intimate Friends

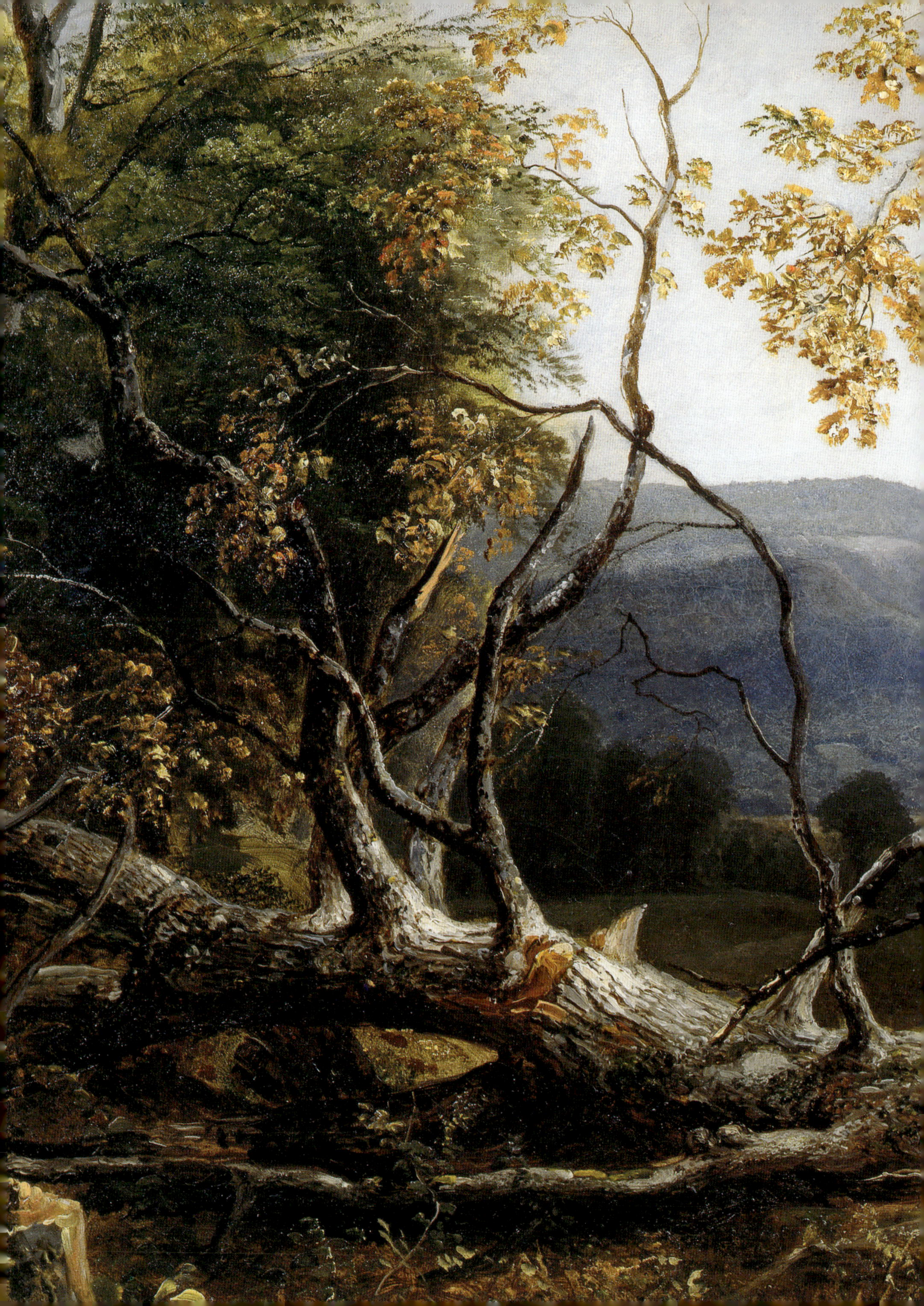

Intimate Friends

Thomas Cole
Asher B. Durand
William Cullen Bryant

Ella M. Foshay and Barbara Novak

The New-York Historical Society

First Edition

Published in conjunction with an exhibition of the same name, held at The New-York Historical Society October 24, 2000, to February 4, 2001

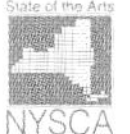

This project is generously supported by the New York State Council on the Arts, a State Agency.

AmericanAirlines
New York's Bridge To The World

American Airlines, the official airline of The New-York Historical Society

Library of Congress Card Number: 00-107402
ISBN 0-916141-04-7

The New-York Historical Society
Two West 77th Street
New York, NY 10024
www.nyhistory.org

Printed in Italy

On the cover: Detail, Asher B. Durand (1796-1886), *White Mountain Scenery, Franconia Notch, New Hampshire*, 1857, oil on canvas. The Robert L. Stuart Collection, on permanent loan from the New York Public Library, Stuart 105

Frontispiece: Detail, Asher B. Durand (1796-1886), *Study from Nature, Stratton Notch, Vermont*, 1853, oil on canvas. Gift of Mrs. Lucy Maria Durand Woodman, daughter of the artist, 1907.21

Table of Contents

Preface

With the opening of the exhibition *Intimate Friends: Thomas Cole, Asher B. Durand and William Cullen Bryant* and the publication of this catalog by co-curators Ella M. Foshay and Barbara Novak, The New-York Historical Society offers a preview of the fine scholarly work it will produce in coming years under the auspices of the new Henry Luce III Center for the Study of American Culture, located on the fourth floor of our landmark building on Central Park West.

The paintings and drawings in *Intimate Friends*, culled primarily from the Historical Society's collection, tell a story about three men who created a new kind of American art in the first half of the nineteenth century—the painters Thomas Cole and Asher B. Durand and the poet and editor William Cullen Bryant. To explore the intellectual exchange among these close friends, the curators have turned to the Historical Society's library for the books, manuscripts and letters they left behind. It is the Historical Society's unique combination of important art collections and rich library holdings that enabled the curators to create this important exhibition.

The Henry Luce III Center for the Study of American Culture, which opens in November 2000, brings out of deep storage more than 40,000 museum objects and places them on public view. Curators and visiting scholars will use the Luce Center as a workshop, to create exhibitions that explore important historical issues.

I am grateful to the curators of *Intimate Friends* for creating a new interpretive setting for one of the Historical Society's great treasures, *The Course of Empire* by Thomas Cole. Ella Foshay's

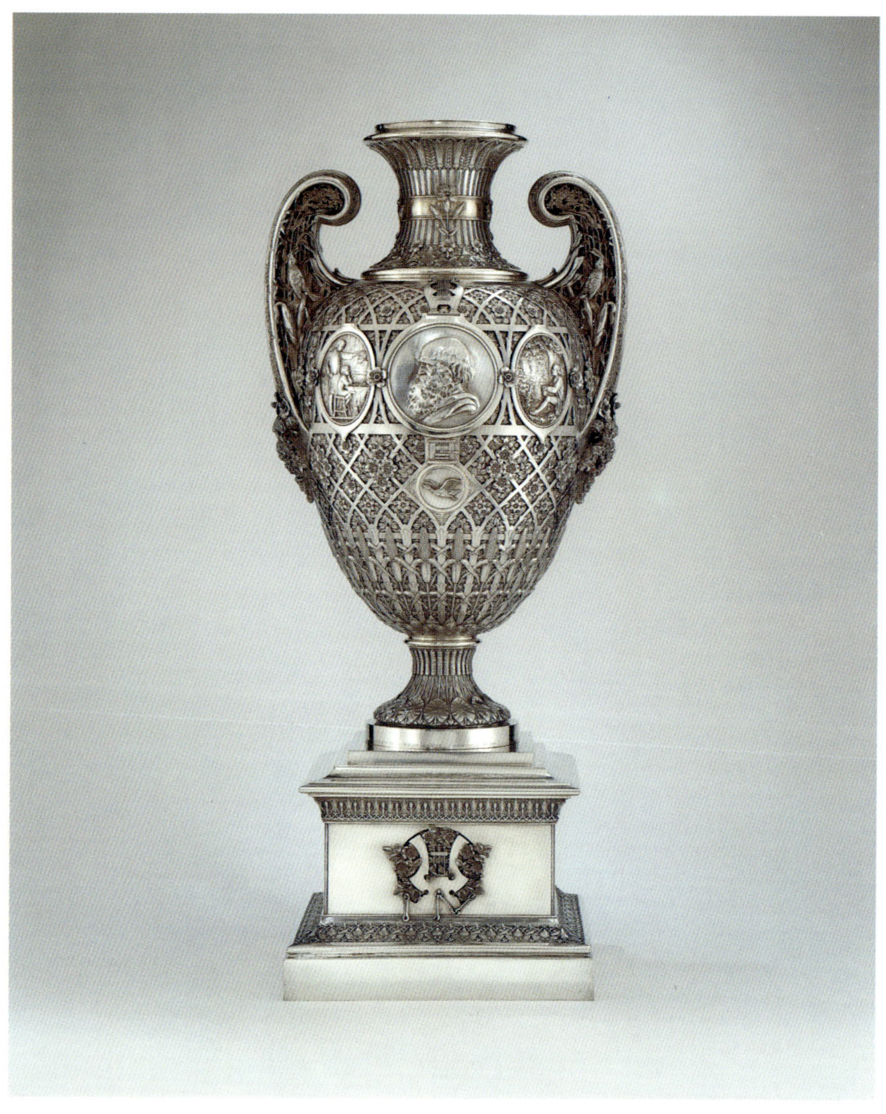

Tiffany & Co., *Presentation Vase, given to William Cullen Bryant by his friends in honor of his eightieth birthday,* 1875-76, silver. Collection of The Metropolitan Museum of Art, Gift of William Cullen Bryant, 1877

exploration of the paintings in relation to Cole and Bryant's shared attraction to the culture of the Old World and nature in the New is especially rewarding. Barbara Novak gives her attention to other great treasures of the collection—the outdoor oil sketches of Durand—and suggests how Durand's pragmatic methodology anticipates both William James and Paul Cézanne.

Many people have worked on this exhibition. I would like to make special mention of exhibition designer Stephen Saitas, design consultant Nello Marconi and catalog editor Nancy Eklund. At the Historical Society, important assistance was provided by Alan Balicki, Glenn Castellano, Stewart Desmond, Paul Gunther, Margaret Heilbrun, Nina Nazionale, Laird Ogden, Jan Seidler Ramirez, Nancy Rosoff, Travis Stewart, Mariam Touba, Grady Turner and Nicole Wells. The research and writing of the catalogue were enhanced by Gloria Gilda Deak, Eagle Glassheim, and Betsy Prioleau. Elizabeth White's contribution to the entire project was invaluable. We are grateful to the following individuals for arranging loans from their institutions: Dr. Annette Blaugrund, Director, and Wendy Rogers, Registrar, of the National Academy of Design; Suzanne L. Shenton, Senior Associate Loans Coordinator, and Peter M. Kenny, Associate Curator of American Art, of the Metropolitan Museum of Art; Rosann Panebianco, Loan Administrator, of the New York Public Library; Russell Flinchum, Archivist, of the Century Association Archives Foundation; and Jonathan Harding, Curator, of the Century Association.

The Historical Society is grateful to Mr. and Mrs. Arthur Altschul for their foresight in proposing an exhibition of our finest paintings to coincide with the opening of the Luce Center. The Overbrook Foundation provided lead sponsorship for *Intimate Friends*. Other funders include the Henry Luce Foundation, the David Schwartz Foundation, the Adelson Galleries, Mrs. and Mrs. Anthony C. Wang, the Spanierman Gallery LLC, the New York City Department of Cultural Affairs, and the New York State Council on the Arts.

Betsy Gotbaum, President
The New-York Historical Society
August 12, 2000

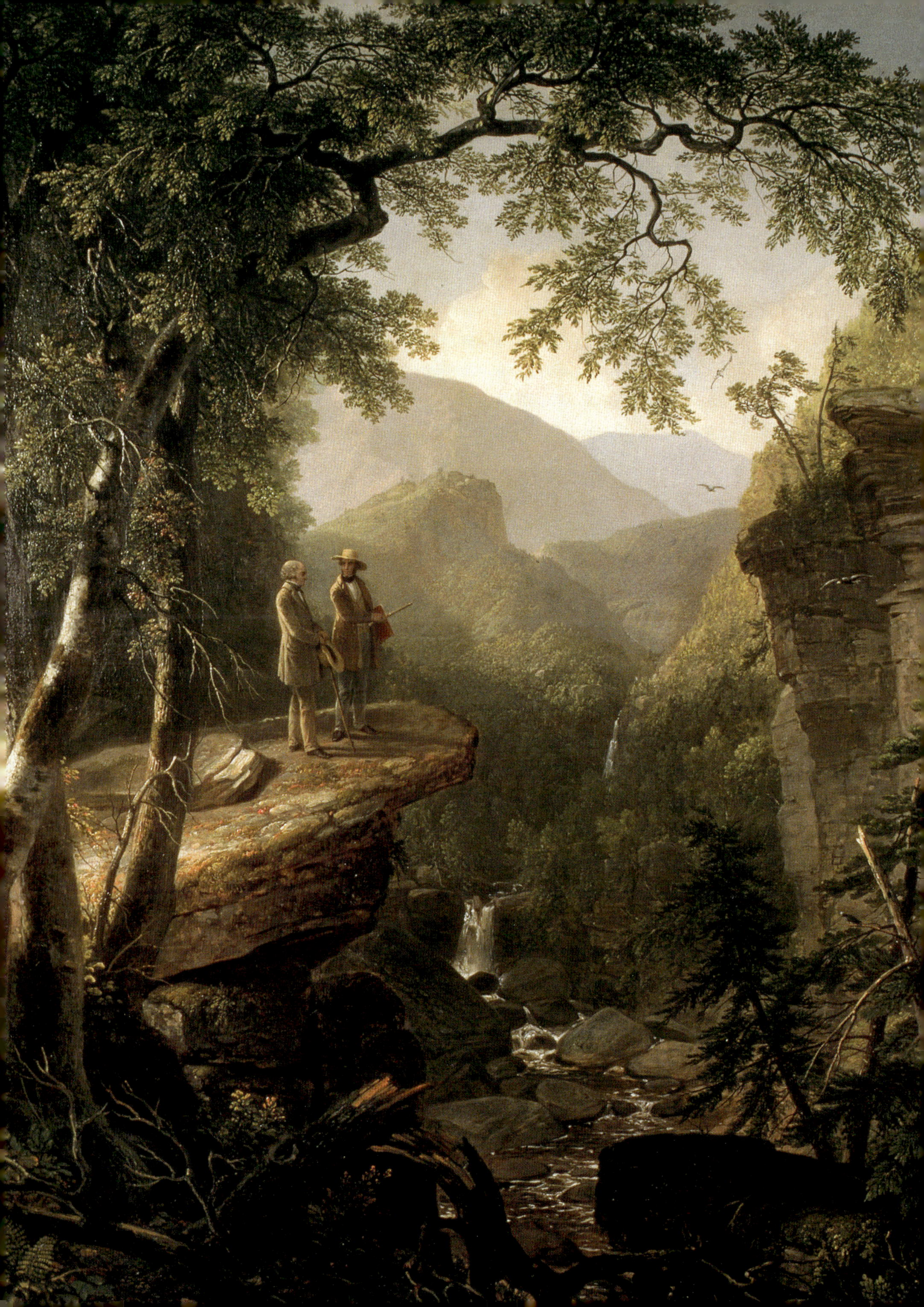

Intimate Friends

Kindred Spirits, a landscape painting by Asher B. Durand (1796-1886), was commissioned as a gift for the poet William Cullen Bryant (1794-1878) in gratitude for the eulogy he delivered in honor of Thomas Cole (1801-1848) at the artist's funeral in 1848. The painting, which therefore embodies the intimate connection of these three men, has become a signature piece of American nineteenth-century art, arguably the most frequently reproduced painting of the period. It deserves this position both literally and figuratively. The artist signed his own name, A. B. DURAND, at the lower left of the canvas when he finished the work in the summer of 1849; but he also cleverly inserted the names THOMAS COLE and WILLIAM CULLEN BRYANT into the picture, by "carving" them in paint on the trunk of the tree in the left foreground. Full-length portraits of the painter Cole and the writer Bryant occupy a commanding position, standing on an outcropping of rock that projects over a ravine. Although only Bryant and Cole appear at the clove in *Kindred Spirits*, clearly all three of the men are there. After all, it was Durand who carved the names of his friends on the tree trunk, delineated the figures, and painted the landscape; he inhabits the setting with every stroke of the brush.[1]

The word "kindred" usually suggests a group of people who are related to one another, or who are of like mind; Bryant, Cole and Durand were, indeed, almost kin. Although lacking blood ties, their personal relationships were close and enduring. Their combined friendships lasted over eighty years. They moved in the same New York circles and belonged to the same clubs; they corresponded, traveled and enjoyed spirited conversation with each other; they were frequent guests at each other's houses. They were also spiritually in tune. The three men shared the belief that nature, particularly nature in the New World, resonated with overtones of

Detail, Asher B. Durand, *Kindred Spirits*, 1849, oil on canvas. Collections, of the New York Public Library, Astor, Lenox, and Tilden Foundations

meaning. It was a sacred place, where true communion could bring not only joy in the beauty of the outdoors, but also enlightenment. With ink and with paint, these artists explored the tangible appearances of the natural world in search of its intangible truths. They communicated their perceptions in landscape paintings and nature poems that guided the direction of cultural ideas and aesthetic expression in nineteenth-century America.

In 1825, the year that the Erie Canal opened promising increased trade and economic prosperity to New York, Bryant and Cole arrived in the city, where they met for the first time. Bryant, a lawyer unhappy with his profession, came to pursue a career in journalism, and Cole, an artist originally from England, came via Ohio seeking patrons. They traveled in the same social circles and became new members of the Bread and Cheese Club, also known as the Lunch Club. This gathering of artists, writers and New York professionals was founded by the novelist James Fenimore Cooper (1789-1851) around 1820. It was probably at the Lunch Club that Bryant and Cole met Asher B. Durand.

Durand had crossed the Hudson River from New Jersey, arriving in Manhattan around 1817 to train in the engraving business. He learned quickly and by 1824 had formed his own firm in partnership with his older brother, Cyrus (1787-1868) called A. B. & C. Durand & Co. The commission, in 1820, from the eminent artist Colonel John Trumbull (1756-1843) to engrave the painter's *Declaration of Independence* gave Durand the prominence to be invited to become one of Cooper's early Lunch Club regulars.[2]

According to Cole's contemporary biographer Louis Legrand Noble, Durand first met Cole on a visit to the painter's Greenwich Street studio in 1825. Trumbull asked Durand to accompany him to look at the work of a young landscape artist, recently arrived in New York. After looking at Cole's paintings, Trumbull is said to have remarked to the artist with admiration, if not envy, "You surprise me, at your age, to paint like this. You have already done, what I, with all my years and experience, am yet unable to do." So impressed were Durand and Trumbull with Cole's work that each came away with a painting under his arm.[3] In 1826, both Cole and Durand helped found the National Academy of Design, a rebel organization governed by artists, founded for the purpose of exhibiting original works by contemporary American painters and sculptors. Lectures on subjects related to the arts were also presented at the National Academy. An Academician as well, Bryant delivered a series of five popular lectures at the National Academy of Design each year, between 1828 and 1831, on Greek and Roman mythology—subjects that would have interested both Cole and Durand.

In 1829, all three men helped found the Sketch Club, an offshoot of the Bread and Cheese Club, which had faded away after its leader, Fenimore Cooper, went off to Europe. The cross-fertilization of ideas in literature and painting was the primary objective of the Sketch Club. Two-thirds of its membership was made up of artists and writers and one-third, of "amateurs," men of diverse occupations—publishers, inventors, manufacturers, merchants—who shared an interest in culture. The club brought together artists and patrons in informal, Friday evening meetings held biweekly at different members' houses. Along with lively conversation, the gatherings involved impromptu sketching of subjects from literature and the writing of verse on topics provided by the host. The interchange of ideas and practice brought such "paper spoilers" as Cole and Durand and literary members like Bryant into a community of friendship and lively debate. Luman Reed was one of a number of merchants who developed collections of American art as a result of their exposure to the painters and writers at the Sketch Club. Reed's early financial support of Cole and Durand was essential to the development of these artists' careers.[4]

Within this congenial social and artistic community, joint ventures between artists and writers were planned and published. Bryant invited Cole and Durand in 1829 to submit work to a literary annual called *The Talisman*. Containing short essays, stories, poems and illustrations, *The Talisman* was started in 1827 by Bryant and two other Sketch Club members, George C. Sands, editor of the *Commercial Advertiser*, and Gulian C. Verplanck, congressman from New York. These collaborations alternated in giving dominance to the writers or the illustrators; sometimes artists were invited to illustrate literary submissions and other times writers were asked to complement images in prose or verse. In the third and final issue of *The Talisman*. Bryant published a sonnet, "To Cole the Painter on his Departure for Europe," bidding farewell to his friend on the eve of the artist's first trip to Europe. Bryant beseeched Cole to maintain his allegiance to the pristine aspect of the American landscape in spite of the "fair scenes" he would encounter in Europe.

> Thine eyes shall see the light of distant skies
> Yet, Cole, thy heart shall bear to Europe's strand
> A living image of thy native land,
> Such as on thine own glorious canvass lies.
> Lone lakes—savannahs where the bison roves—
> Rocks rich with summer garlands—solemn streams—
> Skies where the desert eagle wheels and screams—
> Spring bloom and autumn blaze of boundless groves.
> Fair scenes shall greet thee where thou goest—fair,
> But different—every where the trace of men,
> Paths, homes, graves, ruins, from the lowest glen
> To where life shrinks from the fierce Alpine air.
> Gaze on them, til the tears shall dim thy sight;
> But keep that earlier, wilder image bright.[5]

Bryant welcomed Cole back to America in 1832, this time in prose. He boasted in an editorial in the *New York Evening Post*, where he served as editor, that the United States had artists "equal to any in Europe." The American landscape, he argued, rivaled that of the Old World as a source of artistic inspiration. "We have mountains and clouds, earth and skies as fitted to inspire the poet or the painter as Italy can boast."[6] Bryant promoted the work of American artists in the pages of his newspaper. Like Cole and Durand, Bryant participated in the nationalistic spirit of the Jacksonian period. The desire to create a national culture commensurate with American achievements in democratic governance and economic prosperity found expression in editorials, aesthetic criticism and even the popularity of American subjects in literature and painting.[7]

Working to dispel a feeling of cultural inferiority, these men sought through their writing and painting to embellish and dignify the New World with a culture sown on native soil. The resource that they identified to inspire this native art was the American landscape—unique in its richness, variety and wildness. They emphasized scenery that minimized such intrusions of civilization as railroads, buildings and farmlands. This land was God's creation, still fresh from his hand. It offered spiritual and moral possibilities, these men believed, for those trained to recognize them.

Cole shared with Bryant a poetic imagination and literary bent. He wrote more than one hundred poems, none of which were published during his lifetime. It is doubtful that he intended them for publication, since many are personal responses to topical events, almost like diary entries, and others are left in an unfinished state.[8] One of Cole's poems, expressing the importance to the traveler of the connection with family and friends at home, seems an indirect response to Bryant's farewell sonnet. Cole sympathized with the wretched traveler who goes abroad alone without the support of friends like Bryant to acknowledge his departure and await his return. "Whose wanderings are alike unmark'd—unknown / By Mother, Sister, Wife, by any loving one," wrote Cole.[9]

On the cover of a sketchbook that Cole used during his European trip, Cole penned an untitled poem, dated 1829, that appears to be a direct response to Bryant's exhortation to remember the pristine quality of American natural settings, to "keep that earlier wilder image bright." Cole's poem reads, "Let not the ostentation gaud of art, / That tempts the eye, but touches not the heart, / Lure me from nature's purer love divine."[10] That he carried these lines with him, through the Circean galleries and landscapes of Europe, as a reminder to maintain the purity of his native eye, indicates that Cole shared with Bryant an apprehension of Old World seduction. Its magnetism required self-restraint and discipline. Every time that Cole opened his sketchbook, the poem would caution him to remain faithful to his earlier, purer perception.

In spite of Cole's determination to avoid the temptations of European civilization, and Bryant's warning to his friend to preserve his unspoiled vision of the American landscape, both men were deeply devoted to and nourished by European culture and scenery, particularly that of Italy. Cole and Bryant made two trips to Italy in the 1830s and 1840s, but they did not travel together. Cole preceded Bryant each time by a few years. For both men, these trips merely enhanced an already strong attachment to the historical and artistic traditions of the Old World.

In 1831, after visiting England and France, Cole arrived in Florence, where he spent time painting furiously both indoors and out. He made copies of works in the magnificent galleries of art there and captured views of the historic natural settings in and around the city. Following in Cole's footsteps in 1834, Bryant viewed the landscapes of Italy through the painter's eye. From his hotel room in Florence, the poet saw the river Arno flowing through a landscape by Cole. "The bridge over the Arno, immediately under my window, is the spot from which Cole's landscape...was taken," writes Bryant to a friend. He continues:

> It gives, you may recollect, a view of the Arno traveling off towards the west, its banks overhung with trees, the mountain ridges rising in the distance, and above them the sky flushed with the colors of sunset. The same rich hues I behold every evening in the quarter where they were seen by the artist when he made them permanent on his canvas.[11]

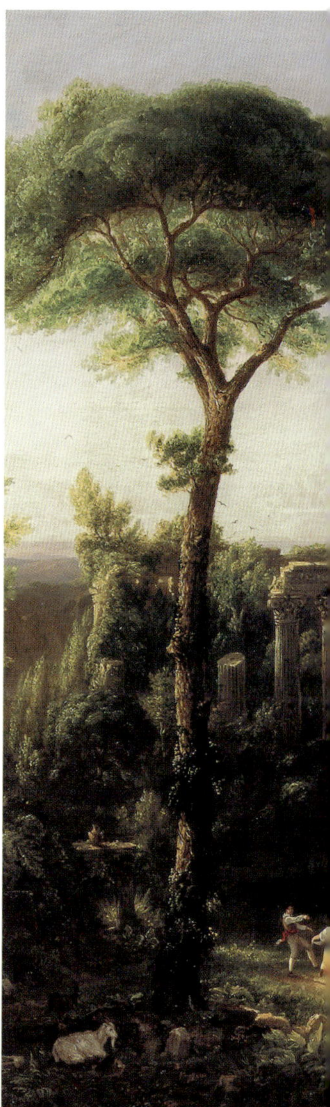

En route from Florence to Rome, Cole determined to enlarge his portfolio of Italian landscapes and "fill [his] sketchbooks with abundant material for future pictures."[12] In Rome, it was the antiquities that fascinated Cole most. The ruins of Roman structures resonated with historical associations. They were concrete embodiments of the past. Strewn around the Italian *campagna*, they called up, in their state of disintegration, the rise and fall of earlier cultures. This idea found poetic expression in British

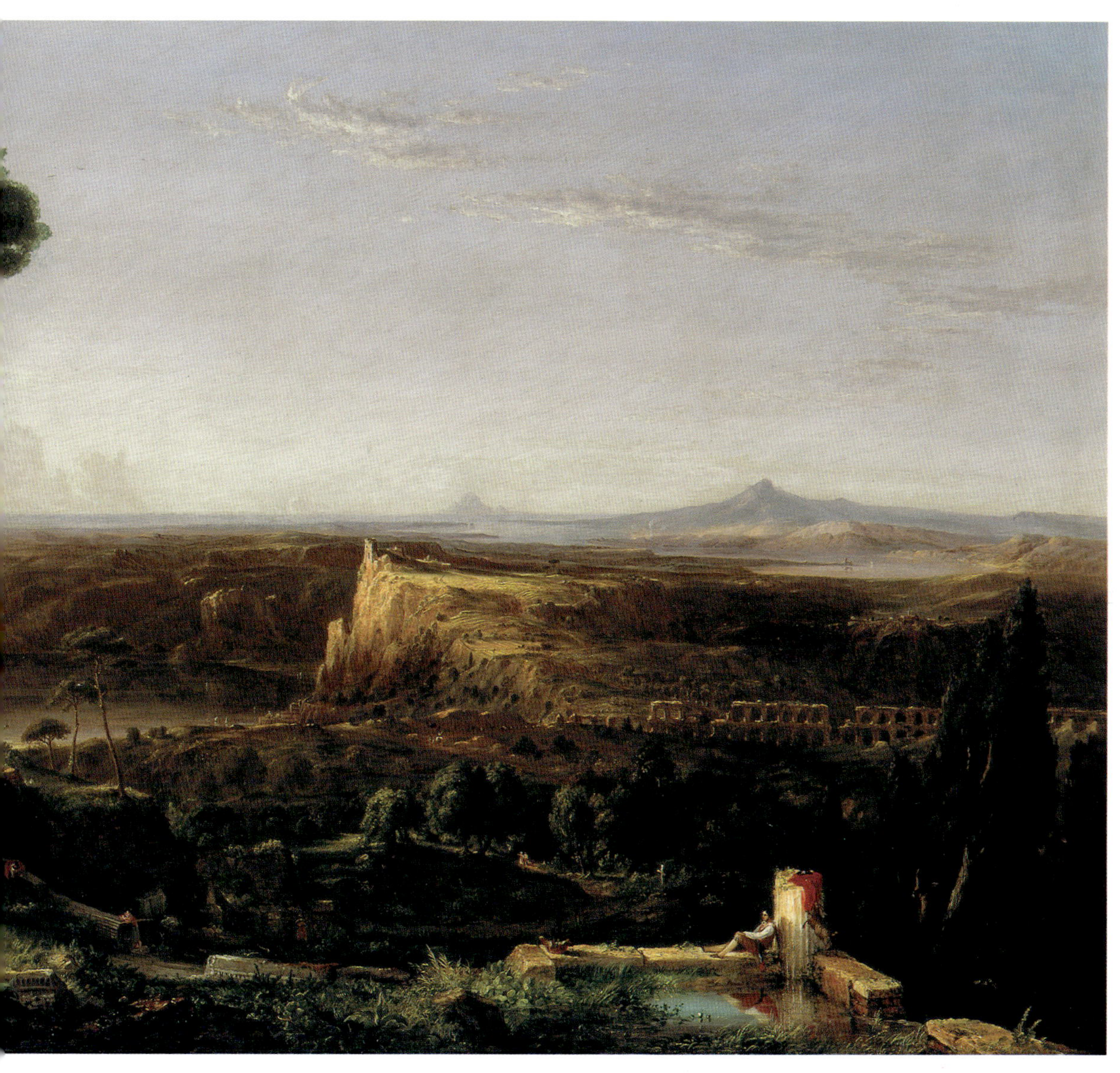

Thomas Cole, *Italian Scene Composition*, 1833, oil on canvas.
Gift of the New-York Gallery of Fine Arts, 1858.19

romantic poetry. Lord Byron, a favorite of Cole's, published *Childe Harold's Pilgrimage; A Romaunt* between 1812 and 1818, which included a melancholy evocation of the ruins of the Roman Empire that had become so popular by the 1830s that it served as a poetic guidebook for travelers of the period and probably for Cole as well.[13]

As the artist's biographer has remarked, "the great difference between Italian scenery and all other, with which he was acquainted, lay, with Cole, less in its material than in its moral and historic elements. Hitherto he had walked with nature in her maidenhood, her fair proportions veiled in virgin robes, affianced indeed to human associations, but unpolluted, unwasted by human passion. But now he was in converse with her, after long centuries of marriage with man."[14] In Italy, Cole took inspiration from the historical and poetic associations of the terrain embedded centuries earlier and developed into maturity through subsequent civilizations. America did not lack symbolic resonance, but the character and age of the symbolism were different. "The great struggle for freedom has sanctified many a spot," wrote Cole in 1835, "and many a mountain, stream, and rock has its legend, worthy of poet's pen or the painter's pencil." But, he concluded, "American associations are not so much of the past as of the present and future."[15]

Italian Scene. Composition, a bucolic view of the Italian countryside, was painted by Cole in New York in 1833 from sketches he brought back with him from Italy. It reflects in its aura of enchanted reverie Cole's affection for both the landscape and history of Italy. "Indeed, to speak of Italy is to recall the desire to return to it," he asserted.[16] Architectural remnants signaled the artistic achievements of classical civilizations. They stood as both witness and reminder. "The glorious scenes of the old world," wrote Cole in his 1835 "Essay on American Scenery," with its "vestiges of antiquity," resonate with associations. Cole saw the landscape of Italy as a "theatre of human events." The ruins conjured up for the artistic imagination the heroic deeds and cultural accomplishments of ancient civilizations, "over which time and genius have suspended an imperishable halo."[17] The same nostalgia for the evocative landscape and ancient Roman ruins of Italy found expression in Cole's poem entitled "The Painter's Lamentation": "And Rome was at my feet, but far below, / Its ruined heaps still sparkling in the glow / Of the unfading sun, which shone as bright / As in the conquering Carthaginians' sight."[18]

Before his first European journey in 1834, Bryant wrote a number of poems that also explored the associative power of the ancient world, such as "The Ages" and "The Greek Boy." In "The Greek Boy," written in New York in 1828, he conjured up the isolated stone remains of a once-great civilization. The valorous men of Greece—triumphant in war, founders of the Olympic games—whose philosophy and literature laid the foundation of Western thought, are gone. Their physical remains are destroyed but have not entirely disappeared. They have returned to nature in the form of dust in the wind and decay in the earth. Man is part of nature's life cycle. He is integrated in the enduring vitality of nature, symbolized by myrtle trees and flowers in bloom. The works of man are ephemeral in comparison with those of nature.

> Gone are the glorious Greeks of old,
> Glorious in mien and mind;
> Their bones are mingled with the mould,
> Their dust is on the wind;
> The forms they hewed from living stone
> Survive the waste of years, alone,
> And, scattered with their ashes, show
> What greatness perished long ago
>
> Yet fresh the myrtles there; the springs
> Gush brightly as of yore;
> Flowers blossom from the dust of kings,
> As many an age before.[19]

That Bryant's reverence for classical culture was established before his first European trip is not surprising. He had studied Latin and Greek literature during his youth in Cummington, Massachusetts. By the age of fourteen, Bryant had read the *Aeneid*, the works of Virgil and the *Orations* of Cicero in Latin. But Greek was his real love. Later, he recalled that, as a boy, he devoted his "whole soul to

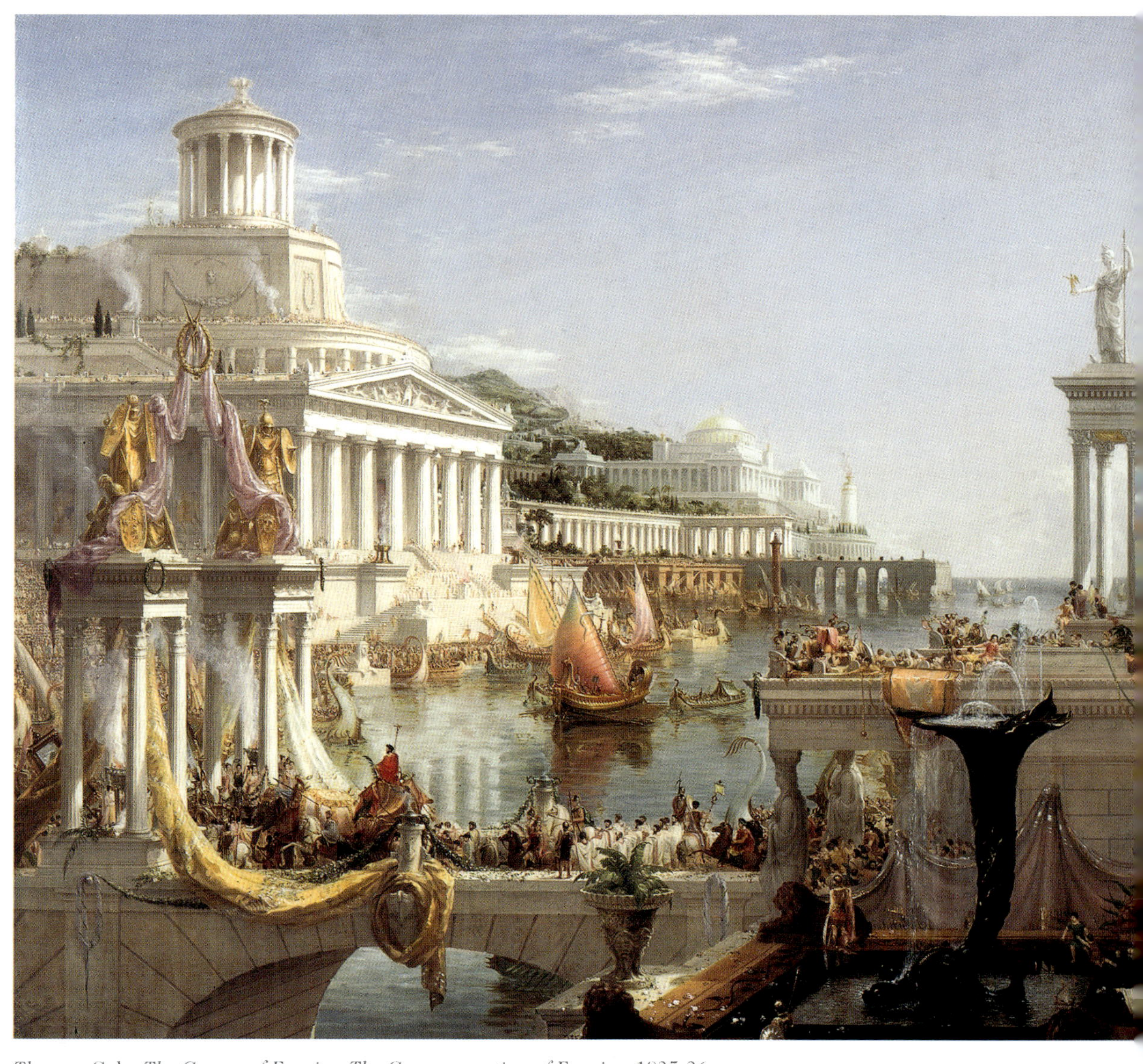

Thomas Cole, *The Course of Empire: The Consummation of Empire*, 1835-36, oil on canvas. Gift of the New-York Gallery of Fine Arts, 1858.3

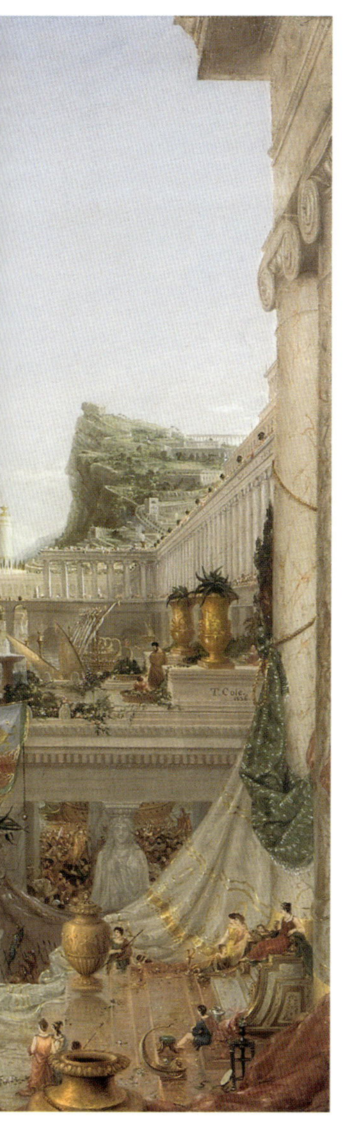

the study of Greek. At night I dreamed of Greek, and my first thought in the morning was of my lesson for the day. At the end of two calendar months I knew the Greek New Testament from end to end."[20] The boy's love of the poetry and language of the ancient Greeks continued throughout Bryant's life: in 1870, he responded to a questionnaire from the Century Association, creating a "mental photograph" of himself. He cited the *Apollo Belvedere* as his favorite sculpture and Homer among his favorite poets.[21]

Bryant began to write, as well as read, poetry. At about seventeen years of age, he wrote most of the poem that has remained his best known and admired ever since. Inspired by his veneration of Greek culture, he titled it "Thanatopsis," which can be translated from the Greek as "contemplation of death." The poem first appeared in an 1817 issue of *The North American Review*. However, "Thanatopsis" was continually revised by Bryant over a period of years, until it was again published in an 1821 collection of poems, some of which indicate his developing interest in the contemplation of nature as a source of spiritual enlightenment rather than a meditation on mortality.

In "Thanatopsis," the young poet considers the stark inevitability of death. He recognizes that the young, the old, the patriarchs, the good, and "the hoary sees of ages past" will eventually be united from their various times and places in death. They will lie down together in the "mighty sepulchre" of nature. Bryant uses precise images to portray the rich beauty of nature's sounds and appearance, a paradoxical beauty that serves to disguise the universal grave:

> The hills
> Rock-ribbed and ancient as the sun,—the vales
> Stretching in pensive quietness between;
> The venerable woods—rivers that move
> In majesty, and the complaining brooks
> That make the meadows green; and, poured round all,
> Old Ocean's gray and melancholy waste,—
> Are but the solemn decorations all
> Of the great tomb of man.[22]

Bryant included a moral lesson in the poem that proceeded from the symbol of nature as an exquisite sarcophagus. "To him who in the love of Nature holds communion with her visible forms," wrote Bryant, "she speaks a various language." Nature can speak to those who seek to hear how to lead a meaningful life and, thereby, approach the grave "like one who wraps the drapery of his couch about him, and lies down to pleasant dreams." Bryant extracted moral ideas from the beauties of nature, the hills, the meadows, the brooks, the ocean. These natural features of the landscape became *memento mori*, or reminders of death. Their beauty is both tangible and symbolic. As reminders of transience, the gems of the natural world encouraged a moral life. For Bryant, the connection between poetry and morality was essential. "Among the most remarkable of the influences of poetry," wrote Bryant in 1824, "is the exhibition of those analogies and correspondences which it beholds between the things of the moral and natural world."[23] Later poems by Bryant imbued nature with codes of moral comportment as well as the possibility of offering a spiritual connection with God. In "A Forest Hymn," the "mighty sepulchre" of nature became "God's ancient sanctuary." It was created long before the artifacts of man; in Bryant's words, "the groves were God's first temples." A place of meditation and communion with God, "Nature, here, In the tranquillity that thou dost love, / Enjoys thy presence."[24]

With classical poetry and prose inculcated in his spirit, it was inevitable that Bryant would greatly admire Thomas Cole's most ambitious historical landscape work, five paintings devoted to the theme of the rise and fall of an ancient classical culture. "The paintings of the *Course of Empire* are among the most remarkable and characteristic of Cole's work. The subject is finely conceived," wrote Bryant, "and though the execution of each is not equal, they have all some peculiar excellence."[25] Executed between 1836 and 1838, Cole's *Course of Empire* is the artist's fullest expression of his ideas about the relationship of civilization—the work of human construction—and nature, the work of divine creation.

With the support of Luman Reed, Cole embarked on the most ambitious set of symbolic compositions of the day. He envisioned for his patron a group of five or more paintings "that should illustrate the History of a natural scene as well as be an Epitome of Man, showing the natural changes of Landscape & those affected by man in his progress from Barbarism to Civilization, to Luxury, to the Vicious state or state of Destruction, and to the state of Ruin & Desolation."[26] The first scene was to be "a savage wilderness" set at sunrise, followed by a representation of early agriculture in a "pastoral" setting in early morning. The third would be "a great City, gorgeous piles of Architecture, Bridges, Aqueducts, Temples & c. (port crowded with vessels, splendid processions under the brilliant light of noonday sun...)" The fourth, an afternoon landscape, would describe a "tempest—a Battle—the burning of the City," and the concluding picture, the city in ruin, back-lit by the setting sun. Cole worried that his conceptions could be too grandiose for his audience: "[They might] smile at my Castles in the Air... I may disappoint myself, as is frequently the case, and find that the living pictures of the mind, in the attempt to embody them, may be transmuted into lifeless clay."[27]

Like Bryant, and possibly with the poet's encouragement, Luman Reed regarded the artist's ideas with respect. A down-to-earth man from Coxackie, New York, who lacked the classical education of Bryant and who did not travel abroad, Reed had little interest in lofty ideas, complex iconography and classical settings. He preferred simple, contemporary local subjects. He wanted them to be recognizable and painted with clarity and finish. "A cat well painted," wrote Reed, "is better than a Venus badly done."[28]

Cole's five paintings trace the rise and fall of an ancient classical civilization. The events take place within a single landscape setting. According to Cole's conception, the changes in weather, time of day and season would provide correspondences in nature to the variety of scenes describing the progress of civilization. The mid-day sun in a clear blue sky, threaded with wispy clouds, illuminates the central and largest painting, depicting the

Consummation of Empire. The artistic accomplishments of classical civilization, in the form of architecture and sculpture, claim pride of place and scale in this canvas. The "piles of architecture" are so massive that they become both the subject and the background of the painting. Perhaps the artist is suggesting that the "Epitome of Man" is not to be found in military might, but in artistic achievement. The ancient world achieved aesthetic excellence, and the ruins, which represent this cultural climax, continued to inspire Cole's painting throughout his life. In a similar fashion, classical poetry provided a stimulus to the literary imagination of William Cullen Bryant into his seventies, when he translated the *Iliad* and the *Odyssey* of Homer into blank verse.

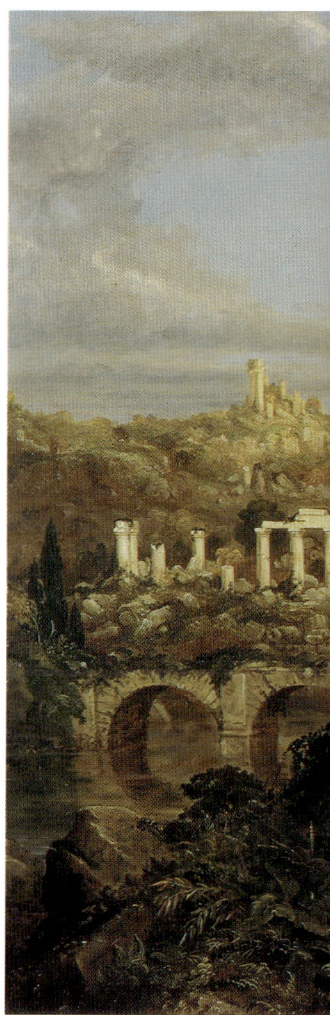

Nature at twilight provides the ambiance for *Desolation*, Cole's final picture in the *Course of Empire* series. Only remnants of classical architecture survive in the form of a single Corinthian column in the left foreground, an aqueduct, and a portion of an arcade fading into the horizon of a moonlit autumn evening. Cole's attraction to moonlight imagery was inspired, in part, by the poetry of Byron, who was also much admired by Bryant. In connection with the exhibition of another moonlight scene, the artist quoted Byron's *Parasina* (1816), which describes the light-dark paradox of a moonlit sky, "that clear obscure / So softly dark and pure / Which follows the decline of day / As twilight melts beneath the moon away."[29] This same time of day envelops the last scene in the *Course of Empire* cycle, and what better time to describe the fall of civilization, an inevitable, yet confounding consequence of greatness?

By the time Cole painted it, this last work may well have had a personal as well as a moral purpose. It was completed in the fall of 1836, a few months after the death of Luman Reed. At that time, Cole wrote a poem in tribute to the memory of his beloved patron. The conclusion of his "Lines occasioned by the death of Mr. Luman Reed" draws a parallel between the life cycle of a man and the passage of a day:

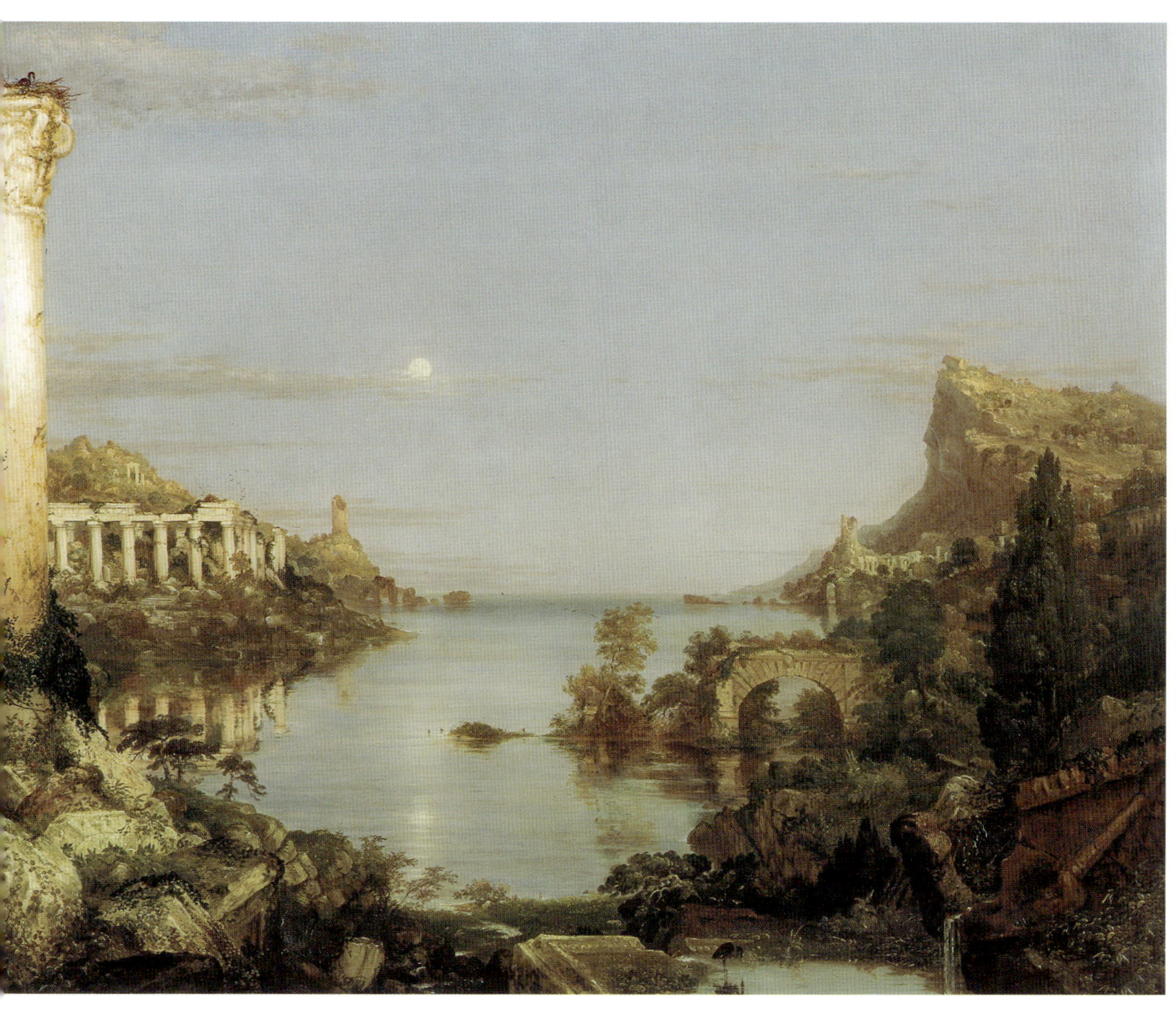

Thomas Cole, *The Course of Empire: Desolation*, 1836, oil on canvas.
Gift of the New-York Gallery of Fine Arts, 1858.5

Thy life of peace
Was like the summer cloud that rose at morn
To grace the earth and as the day advanced
Increased in beauty; til the setting sun
Wrapp'd it in splendour ere the night was come.[30]

Cole sent a copy of his poetic tribute to Reed to Asher B. Durand, whose artistic career also was launched by the patron. It was Reed who provided Durand the necessary financial support to give up engraving in favor of painting. He commissioned him to paint portraits of the five presidents of the United States for his collection and went on to purchase some of Durand's earliest paintings in the narrative genre. Indeed, Reed died an untimely death at the age of fifty-one, leaving behind a devoted group of artists as well as a substantial collection of American paintings; that collection was to play a significant role in encouraging other wealthy men to support contemporary American artists. So important was Reed's support of these men and others that Bryant called him "one of the most generous and judicious friends of art whom the country ever had."[31]

Although Cole's literary imagination drew him to depict thematic landscape compositions, he also painted more intimate views of natural settings in the Catskills, Vermont and New Hampshire. From pencil drawings of sites, made in his sketchbooks on long walks through the landscapes of New England and New York, Cole composed paintings of local views in his studio. *Sunset, View on the Catskill*, of 1834, depicts an actual place that Cole liked to visit on his ramblings through the Catskills in summertime. It is a view of North Mountain seen from Catskill Creek. This is one of many sunset and twilight scenes that Cole painted, drawn to the time of day when the fading light cloaked the facts of nature in mystery, giving poetic overtones to the landscape. In gazing on such a sunset scene in a "favored region," a man experienced not only a sensation of pleasure, "that passes with the occasion leaving no trace behind," wrote Cole in his 1836 "Essay on American Scenery," "but in gazing on the pure creations of the Almighty, he feels a calm religious tone steal through his mind."[32] The experience of spiritual communion with nature similarly affected Cole's friend Bryant, and he expressed it in many of his verses. The poem "A Walk at Sunset" evokes the fading, low lights of the evening sun as inspiration to sing praise to God:

> When insect wings are glistening in the beam
> Of the low sun, and mountain-tops are bright,
> Oh, let me, by the crystal valley-stream
> Wander amid the mild and mellow light;
> And while the wood-thrush pipes his evening lay
> Give me one lonely hour to hymn the setting day.[33]

In July of 1840, Bryant and Cole took a trip through the Catskills, walking on some days from dawn to dusk. In the course of their wanderings, they gave names to various sites, some of which still carry those names today. They both enjoyed the great variety of landscape vistas, casting their eyes, as Bryant remembered in 1848, "over scenes of wild grandeur peculiar to our country, over our aerial mountain-tops with their mighty growth of forest never touched by the axe, along the banks of streams never deformed by culture, and into the depth of skies bright with the hues of our own climate."[34] Cole and Bryant also spent time observing the details of the landscapes through which they walked. Trees, mossy banks, and small streams invited close observation. Bryant could identify without difficulty most of the plant species by their Latin name. Instructed in Linnaean botany in his youth by his father, he wrote a practical treatise on plants that was published in Cordelia Harris Turner's book *The Floral Kingdom* in 1896.[35]

On the 1840 trip, Bryant admired firsthand the acuity of Cole's eye for the details of nature. He understood, however, that the observations made by Cole during these walks were not transferred in their raw state to the artist's canvas. Because the vivid images haunted Cole with their distinctness, he found that he could not successfully paint a scene immediately upon return from a walk. He had no interest in transcribing direct experience. The scenes recorded by his mind's eye had to be digested and distilled into

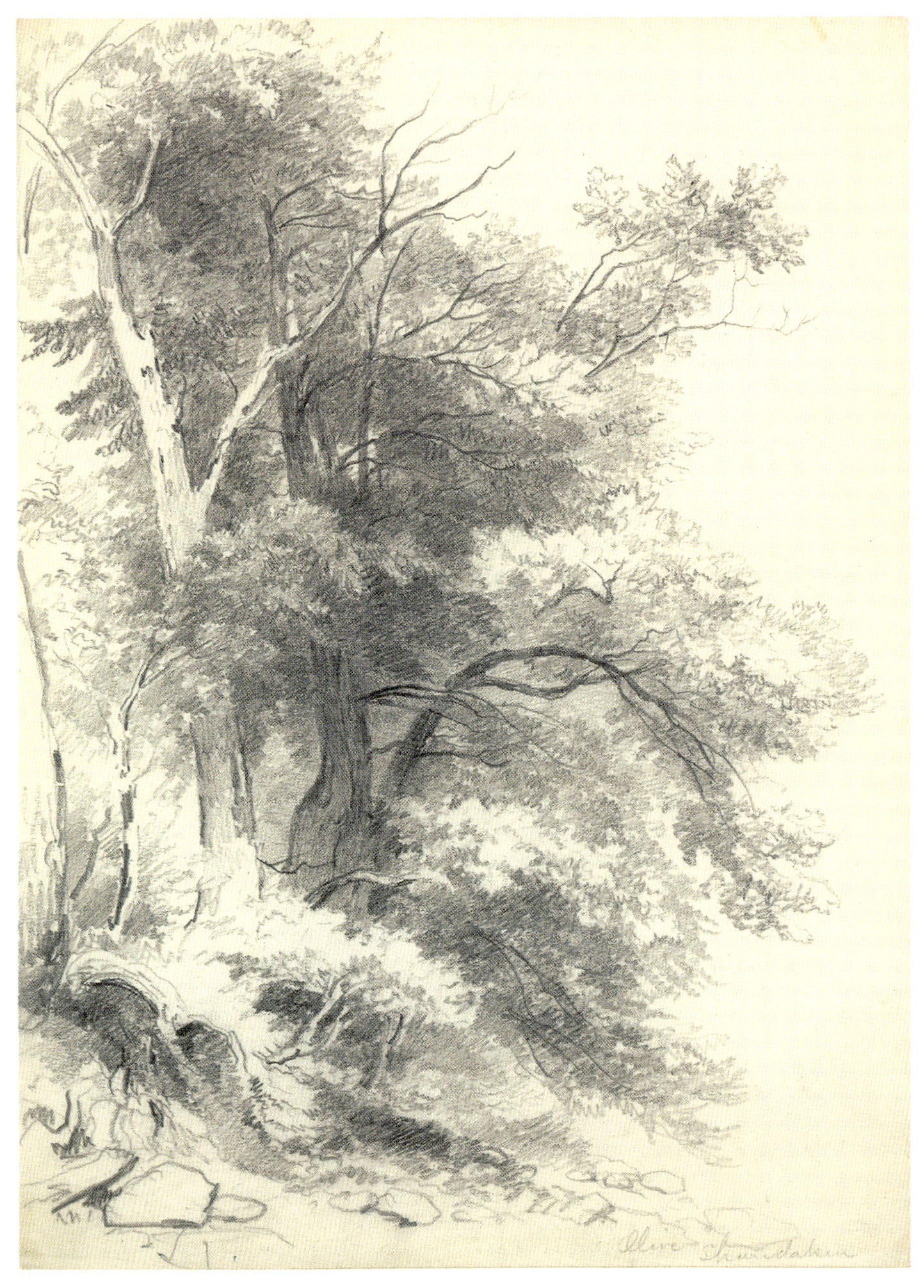

Asher B. Durand, *Study of Trees, Shandaken, New York,* not dated, pencil on paper. Gift of Miss Nora Durand Woodman, granddaughter of the artist, 1918.260

ideal form after the passage of time. "I must wait for time to draw a veil over the common details, the unessential parts, which shall leave the great features, whether the beautiful or the sublime, dominant in the mind," said Cole.[36]

Unlike his mentor and friend, Cole, Durand was attracted to the "common details" of nature, spotted *in situ*. He sought to study them with a clear eye and reproduce them faithfully. He did not want to lose the keenness of his first impression. Durand noted down with pencil and with paint the particulars of nature. On his walks through the woods, he made oil sketches of rocky banks, small groups of trees, and gentle streams. These spontaneous oil sketches made *en plein air* convey both the look and feel of direct experience. The delicacy of the peeling bark on a fallen, dead tree in *Study from Nature, Stratton Notch, Vermont*, painted in 1853, or the craggy, light-dappled surface of a boulder found in the woods in *Study from Nature: Rocks and Trees*, of 1856, were imprinted with vivid clarity on Durand's visual cortex. The surface textures of these informal subjects found painterly equivalents through his hand. His was a tactile sensibility, far removed from the "castles in the air," spun by the poetic imagination of Cole. The simple design of these studies is also different from the complex compositions of Cole's allegorical landscapes. Durand uses nature in the form of a dead tree or a bunch of rocks to compose the picture. The artist sought to discover design in nature, rather than to rearrange the elements of nature to create a pleasing pictorial design. These spontaneous records of casual sites, represented with respectful precision, are, however, no less imbued with the grandeur of nature than the large-scale landscape compositions orchestrated months later in the artists' city studios.

It was Cole who first encouraged Durand to move away from portrait and genre subjects and begin painting landscapes. After their first meeting in Cole's studio, the two artists developed a close personal friendship during the 1830s. In the summer, they frequently roamed through the Adirondack, Catskill and White mountains together, making sketches to use in their paintings composed indoors in winter. Durand's early landscapes were allegorical, fashioned in the tradition of his mentor Cole. However, these works did not occupy a central place in his *oeuvre*. Although he traveled and sketched in Europe in the early 1840s, the same period that Cole and Bryant wandered in the Catskills, he was disinterested in ruins and only mildly impressed with Italian scenery. He wrote home from Italy that "when all this looking and studying and admiring shall have an end, I am free to confess that I shall enjoy a sight of the signboards in the streets of New York."[37]

The distance from home only made Durand more sharply aware of the extraordinary qualities of American scenery. To his eye, the Swiss Alps paled in comparison to the rocks and meadows of Hoboken, New Jersey. His intimate knowledge of these hometown spots, gained through fishing their streams, made him appreciate them more. In his "Letters on Landscape Painting," published in 1855, Durand advised aspiring landscape artists to let nature be their first and most important mentor. "Go first to Nature to learn to paint landscape," he wrote. A trip to Europe would be nothing more than an unnecessary tangent. "Go not abroad then in search of material for the exercise of your pencil," he warned, "while the virgin charms of our native land have claims on your deepest affections."[38] He was passing on his own love of American scenery, which for him held special beauty. That he expressed these ideas in prose, rather than poetry, was in keeping with his colloquial approach to landscape art. Durand found in nature not only the sources of his artistic approach, but also intimations of the meaning of life. "The external appearance of this our dwelling-place apart from its wondrous structure and functions which minister to our well-being," Durand claimed, "is fraught with lessons of high and holy meaning, only surpassed by the light of Revelation."[39] Wandering through the woods and selecting scenes as he found them was, for Durand, a spiritual journey. The works that he produced became acts of devotion.

Durand's most successful large-scale landscape compositions depict American scenes, not sites in the Italian *campagna*. From sketches in pencil and paint, made out-of-doors since his earliest outings, Durand accumulated a treasury of local landscape features to incorporate in grander landscape compositions. In *White Mountain Scenery, Franconia Notch, New Hampshire* (1857), twenty years of direct interaction with and documentation of nature in sketchbooks coalesced into a panoramic painting that carried the impression of being there at the site. The artist captured both the look and the feel of the place. It was this precise experiential quality of nature that the eminent art critic Henry Tuckerman admired in the painter's work. "We can hear the rustling of the leaves before the pattering of the shower," he wrote in praise of Durand's landscape paintings, "scent the loamy breath of the earth, and feel the exhausted air that precedes the lightening." In a succinct phrase, the critic asserted that, among artists, Durand had "the greatest feeling for nature."[40]

Tuckerman drew many parallels between Durand's painting and the poetry of William Cullen Bryant, remarking that "in spirit they [were] identical."[41] In some cases, the connections between the poet's and the artist's work was direct. In Bryant's poems, Durand found confirmation of his belief that the particulars of nature were the embodiments of God's handiwork. To study these particulars carefully was a process of enlightenment; to recreate them in text and image was a religious endeavor. Durand produced several pictures based on themes from Bryant's verses, including *Thanatopsis* and *Early Morning at Cold Spring*, both painted in 1850. Lines from Bryant's "A Scene on the Banks of the Hudson," written twenty years earlier, inspired Durand to paint the scene at Cold Spring on the Hudson River. Durand sought to express in his painting, as Bryant did in verse, the religious overtones—the "Sabbath bells"—that reverberate in the solitary contemplation of an exquisite river scene:

> Cool shades and dews are round my way.
> A silence of the early day;
> Mid the dark rocks that watch his bed,
> Glitters the mighty Hudson spread.
> Unrippled, save by drops that fall
> From shrubs that fringe his mountain wall;
> And o'er the clear still water swells
> The music of the Sabbath bells.[42]

Like his companions Cole and Bryant, Durand explored nature to find God. He did not, however, get seduced by the scenery of Europe and the antiquities of Italy as essential to his aesthetic and moral education. He was attracted by the present, not the past. Durand could see God's image reflected in the watery glass of the Hudson and hear echoes of His voice in the tinkle of droplets from riverbank shrubs falling on its surface. It was Durand, in fact, who listened closely to the advice that Bryant gave to Cole, but which the poet himself did not always follow; Durand ignored the call of Italy and remained faithful to the mountains and cloves of his own backyard. He fulfilled William Cullen Bryant's contention that the landscape painter had a greater familiarity with nature than the poet. "He studies her aspect more minutely," wrote Bryant. "Not one of her forms is lost upon him; not a gleam of sunshine penetrates her green recesses, not a cloud casts its shadow unobserved by him; every tint of the morning or the evening, of the gray or the golden noon, of the near or the remote object is noted by his eye and copied by his pencil."[43] Durand's *plein air* oil sketches of nature and his landscape compositions based upon them were direct projections of his focus on American scenery, untouched by the ax and unscarred by the works of man. He kept "that earlier, wilder image bright" and endowed his re-creations of its most humble aspects with revelations of the divine. He preserved "the fresh green breast of the New World," an undefiled and optative landscape filled with promise for the future, to be rediscovered by F. Scott Fitzgerald and by other writers and artists in the centuries to follow.

Endnotes

1. Perhaps as a tribute to Thomas Cole, Durand based the landscape setting in *Kindred Spirits* on *Gelyna; View Near Ticonderoga*, painted twenty years earlier by his friend and mentor. Bryant, William Cullen, *Miscellanies: First Published under the Name of The Talisman* 3 (New York: Elam Bliss, 1833), facing page 302.

2. Many of the early connections between Durand, Cole and Bryant can be found in Callow, James T., *Kindred Spirits: Knickerbocker Writers and American Artists, 1807-1855* (Chapel Hill: University of North Carolina Press, 1967), 62-69.

3. Noble, Louis Legrand, *The Life and Works of Thomas Cole* (Cambridge, Mass.: Belknap Press, 1964), 35-36.

4. Callow (1967), 14-19.

5. Bryant 3 (1833), 3.

6. Thomas Cole, cited in Brown, Charles H., *William Cullen Bryant* (New York: Charles Scribner's Sons, 1971), 212. Bryant also arranged a formal address at the Sketch Club to welcome Cole home from Europe.

7. William Cullen Bryant's review of the annual exhibition at the National Academy of Design in the *New York Evening Post* (Saturday, May 9, 1829), 2, for example, applauds these annuals for their contribution to "the progress of the fine arts among us."

8. Thomas Cole's poems were published posthumously, in 1972, by Marshall Tymn, who felt that they complemented the artist's work and provided a fuller portrait of the man and his times. Tymn, Marshall B., ed., *Thomas Cole's Poetry* (York, Penn.: Liberty Cap Books, 1972), 23-24.

9. Tymn (1972), 21.

10. Tymn (1972), 52.

11. Bryant, William Cullen, *Letters of a Traveller; or, Notes of Things Seen in Europe and America*, 3rd ed. (New York: G. P. Putnam, 1851), 24.

12. Noble (1964), 101.

13. Wallach, Alan P., "Cole, Byron and the *Course of Empire*," *Art Bulletin* 50 (December 1968), 375-79.

14. Noble, Louis L., *The Course of Empire, Voyage of Life, and Other Pictures of Thomas Cole* (New York: Cornish Lamport & Co., 1853), 153-54, cited in Novak, Barbara, *The Arcadian Landscape: American Painters in Italy* (Kansas City, Kans.: University of Kansas Museum of Art, 1972), xi.

15. Cole, Thomas, "Essay on American Scenery," *The American Monthly Magazine* n.s. 1 (January 1836), 11.

16. Dunlap, William, *The History of the Rise and Progress of the Arts of Design in the United States* II (New York: George P. Scott, 1834), 363-64.

17. Cole (1836), 4.

18. Tymn (1972), 70.

19. Bryant, William Cullen, *The Poetical Works of William Cullen Bryant* (New York: D. Appleton and Company, 1929), 120.

20. Godwin, Parke, *A Biography of William Cullen Bryant with Extracts from his Private Correspondence* 1 (New York: D. Appleton and Company, 1883), 32-33.

21. Bryant, William Cullen, "Mental Photograph by the Subject," New York, March 1870, Bryant Manuscripts, The Century Association Archives Foundation, New York.

22. Bryant (1929), 22.

23. Bryant, William Cullen, *Lectures on Poetry* (1824), cited in Pearce, Roy Harvey, *The Continuity of American Poetry* (Princeton, N.J.: Princeton University Press, 1961), 206.

24. Bryant (1929), 79-80.

25. Bryant, Willian Cullen, *A Funeral Oration, Occasioned by the Death of Thomas Cole, Delivered Before the National Academy of Design, New-York, May 4, 1848* (New York: D. Appleton & Co., 1848), 23.

26. Thomas Cole to Luman Reed, September 18, 1833, Thomas Cole Papers, New York State Library, Albany, New York.

27. Koke, Richard J., *American Landscape and Genre Paintings in the New-York Historical Society* 1 (New York: New-York Historical Society, 1982), 193-95.

28. Luman Reed to George Flagg, March 9, 1835, Asher B. Durand Papers, New York Public Library, New York.

29. *The Poetical Works of Lord Byron* (London, 1960), 330, cited in Foshay, Ella M., *Mr. Luman Reed's Picture Gallery* (New York: Harry N. Abrams, Inc., 1990).

30. Tymn (1972), 83.

31. Bryant (1848), 24.

32. Cole, Thomas, "Essay on American Scenery," *American Monthly Magazine* 7 (January 1836), 3.

33. Bryant (1929), 37.

34. Bryant (1848), 14.

35. Godwin (1883), 36.

36. Letter from Cole to a "distinguished friend," cited in Bryant (1848), 39.

37. Durand, John, *The Life and Times of A. B. Durand* (1970), 165, cited in Novak, Barbara, *American Painting of the Nineteenth Century: Realism, Idealism and the American Experience*, 2nd ed. (New York: Harper & Row, 1979), 83.

38. Durand, Asher B., "Letters on Landscape Painting," *The Crayon* 1 (January-June 1855), 33-34.

39. Durand (1855), 34.

40. Tuckerman, Henry T., *Book of the Artists: American Artist Life: Comprising Biographical and Critical Sketches of American Artists...* (New York: G. P. Putnam and Sons, 1867), 189.

41. Henry Tuckerman, cited in Lawall, David B., *Asher Brown Durand: His Art and Theory in Relation to His Times* (New York: Garland Publishing Inc., 1977), 468.

42. Bryant (1929), 115.

43. Bryant (1848), 40.

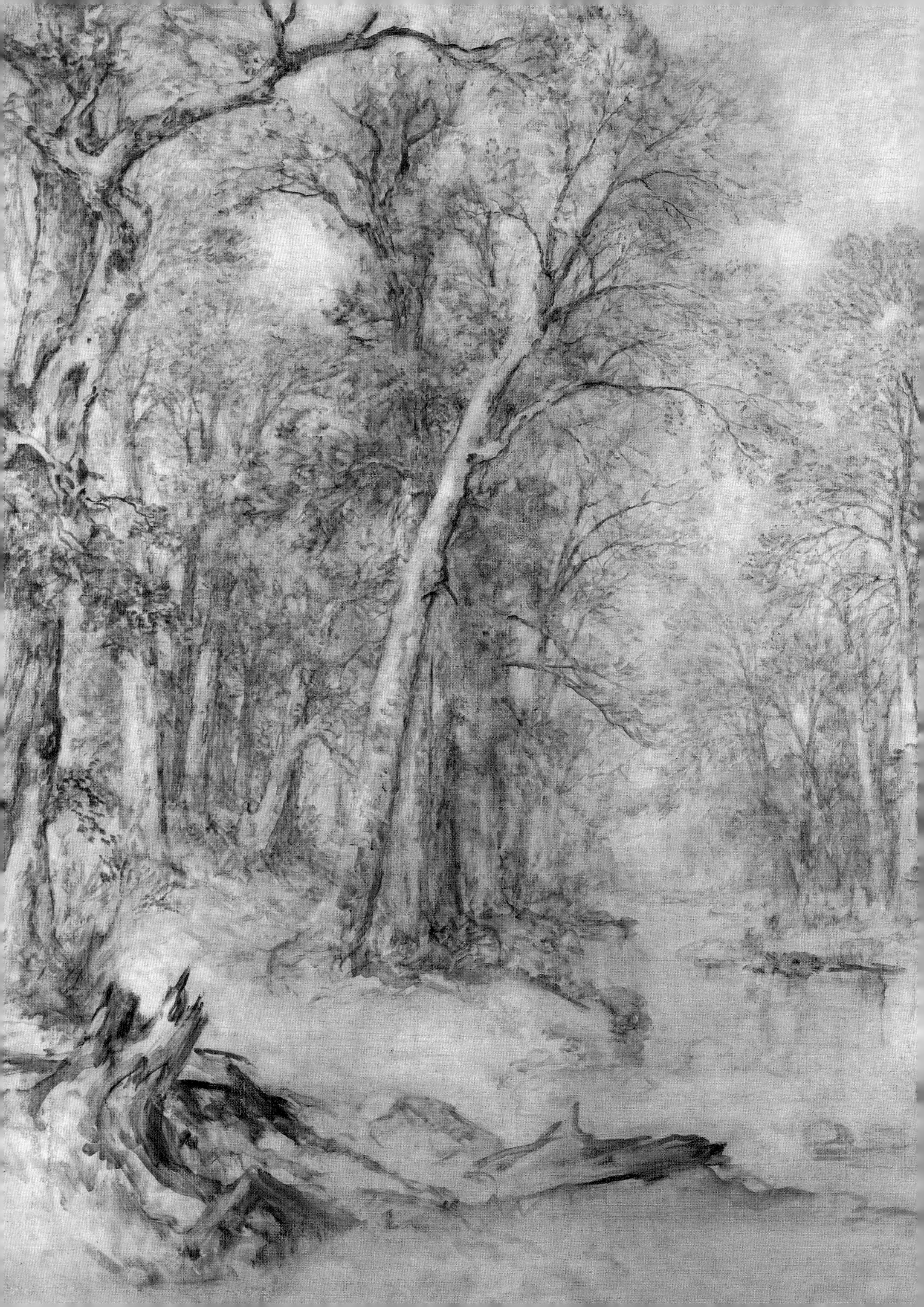

A Note on Durand's *Studies from Nature*

Asher B. Durand (1796-1886) seems an unlikely candidate to represent a nineteenth-century American *avant-garde*, yet that's what he was. He shared with Thomas Cole (1801-1848) and William Cullen Bryant (1794-1878) a belief in nature as a Holy Book, each leaf and branch a page written by Creation. But his pragmatic approach to the natural world aligns him with such revolutionary European painters as Gustave Courbet (1819-1877), even as I will show, with Paul Cézanne (1839-1906)—unexpected comparisons for an American artist in a land where artistic traditions were young, untried and sometimes borrowed.

Cole, Durand's friend and mentor, encouraged him to abandon engraving for painting in the 1830s and to begin by painting the fields of Hoboken, New Jersey, which Durand later referred to—in a letter written on his only European visit in 1840—as "Elysian fields." For most of his life, Cole was torn between nature and culture; like many Europeans he usually deferred to the durable landscape tradition initiated by Claude Lorrain (1604/5-1682). *Course of Empire*, conceived in Italy, is a paean not only to the cyclical nature of civilization but to the trinity of Claude, J. M. W. Turner (1775-1851) and John Martin (1789-1854). Artistic precedents were interfused in Cole's mind with the nature he passionately observed. Durand himself produced his share of Hudson River School paintings in what I have called the "Claudian mode"—the framing trees, the central pond, the foreground coulisse, the far distance, all manicured into a pastoral dream.

Asher B. Durand, *Woodland Brook*, probably 1859, sepia oil on canvas.
Gift of Miss Nora Durand Woodman, granddaughter of the artist, 1930.11

But several of Durand's smaller studies from nature, mostly from the 1850s, break with all previous conventions. Empirical, immediate, alive with the joy of fresh perception, they have a remarkably modern look. The sign of cultural appropriation, the Claudian imprint, is gone. What is "happened upon," seen as if with a casual glance during a walk in the forest, is preserved, "as is." Trees and rocks are not relocated and shifted to accommodate a pre-existing concept, but seen close-up, directly transcribing the artist's pragmatic experience in the American woods.

This, in American art of the period, was a revolutionary artistic act, made possible, one may speculate, by Durand's own practical nature. Though some of his paintings were inspired by Bryant's poems (*Thanatopsis*; *Early Morning at Cold Spring*), his temperament was considerably less literary and intellectual than Cole's. Durand's view of nature was instructed by his sportsman's eye; he is on record as surveying a potential site for its fishing as well as for its painting possibilities. Words and ideas mattered to him far less than they did to Cole.

Cole, after studying nature closely, liked to withdraw, to invite the "veil of memory" to "digest" the scene before painting it. He was haunted by the great artistic traditions that to him spelled "culture." Few of his works were executed in *plein air*. For all its involvement in looking and feeling, Cole's method locates his art in past time, in the contemplative mind. Durand's *Studies from Nature*, produced on the spot, deal forcefully with the moment of experience. Encountering them now, their freshness and vitality announce their "presentness."

Durand's pragmatism aligns him with an American tradition that has not yet been fully recognized, one stemming from Copley's observation of the portrait subject before him. Some of the works of Durand's Hudson River School colleagues are retrieved by this empirical eye. John Frederick Kensett (1816-1872), Jasper Francis Cropsey (1823-1900), Frederic Edwin Church (1826-1900) and Albert Bierstadt (1830-1902) have moments of immediate apprehension and presentation, though never so radically as Durand's.

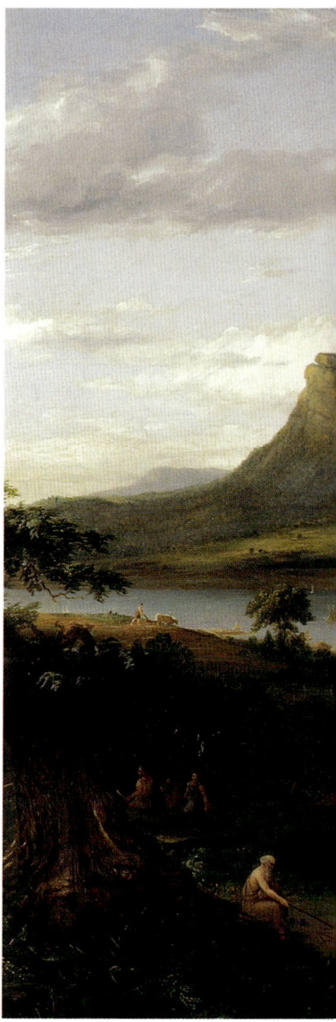

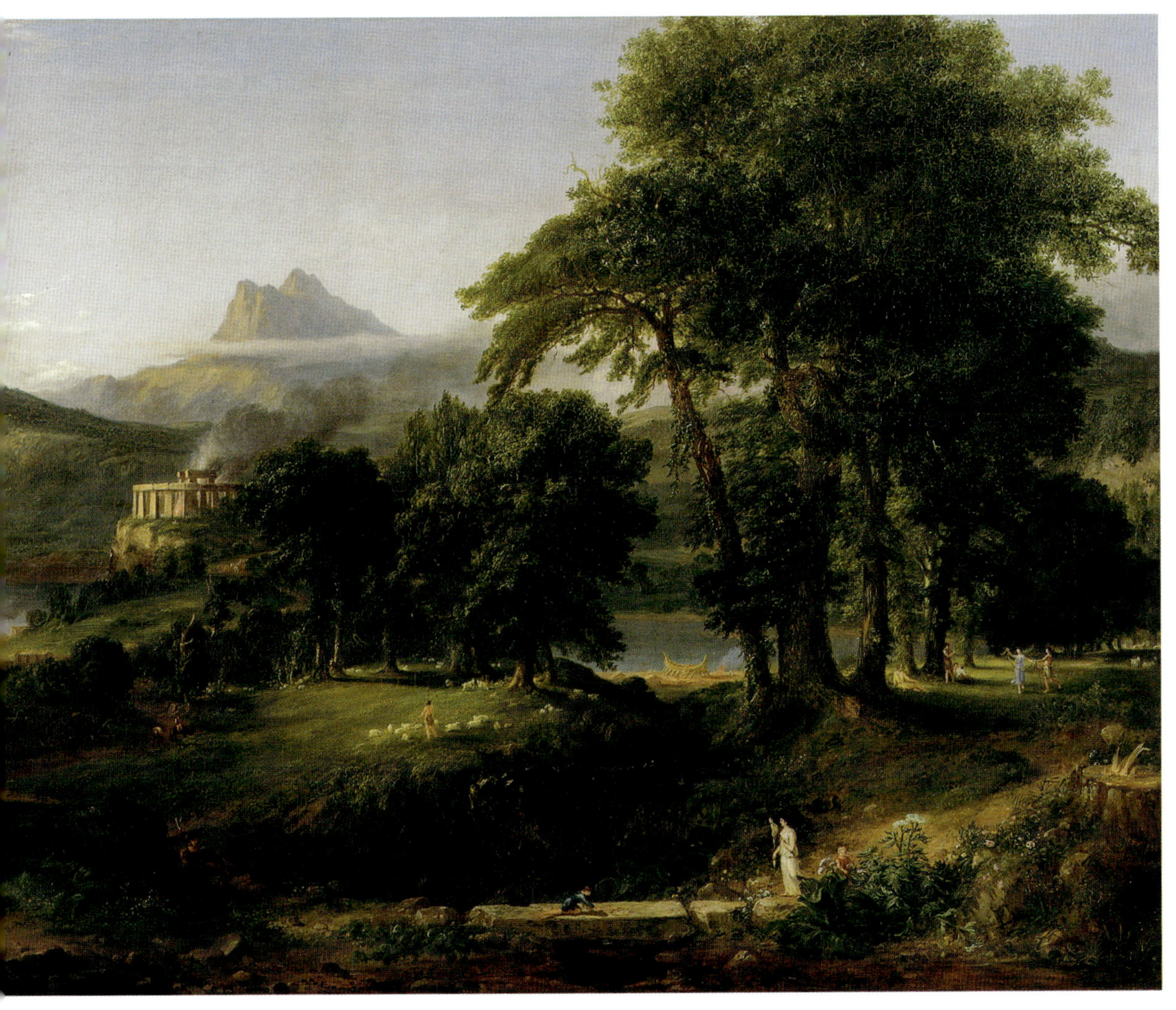

Thomas Cole, *The Course of Empire: The Arcadian or Pastoral State*, not dated, oil on canvas. Gift of the New-York Gallery of Fine Arts, 1858.2

Only Durand painted rocks and trees that can be aligned with those of Courbet and Cézanne, itself a radical suggestion.

My use of the word "tradition" in relation to American art requires some elaboration. I have long maintained that tradition in America involves a curious habit. Certain attitudes and methodologies are not fluently passed from one generation of artists to another, as they are in Europe. Instead, each artist tends instinctively to return to the beginning of a painterly problem, to struggle with it, seeking its resolution on his own terms, as if it had never been tackled before. This sense of difficulty through which each artist authenticates his work amounts to a cultural signature. Individual solutions are often similar because the contextual circumstances of American experience and its predilections are similar.

John Singleton Copley's (1738-1815) American-period pragmatism illustrates the point. The intensity of his direct, moment-to-moment encounter, from the 1750s to mid-1770s, with the specifics of his subject-sitter—the volumes of head, body, garments in space—overrode the conceptual linear patterns of his limner predecessors and the conventions of portraiture derived from his English mezzotint models. Copley's art developed out of his empirical addition of the tactile to his optical sensations—a classic definition of the act of perception. Similarly, in these nature studies Durand's rocks are felt tactilely as well as optically. In an act of fresh and immediate perception, Durand's empiricism shed earlier borrowed conventions. How and why he managed to do so is not mysterious if one refers to the peculiarities of the American tradition described above, and also to his intense study of nature. Durand's program as he wandered in search of subjects has a somewhat casual but directed spontaneity about it. His sportsman's eye was good at noticing informal subjects, pre-selected for their structural potential. The results paralleled similar works by Courbet at around the same time, and, I believe, anticipated those of Cézanne decades later as he, like Cézanne "realized" his sensations. Feeling into the happened-upon volumes of rocks and trees of the American forest, he re-built them into the paintings as Cézanne was to do in Aix-la-Provence.

Like Cézanne, he returned to those trees and rocks over and over again, to elicit their solidity and merge it with the structure of the painting.

Yet similar works do not necessarily imply similar contexts. Cultural experiences in Europe and America differed vastly in the nineteenth century. The artistic climate of mid-nineteenth-century America was not that of late-nineteenth-century France. In the essays contained in "Letters on Landscape Painting," published in *The Crayon* in 1855. Durand made proto-Impressionist observations about "atmospheric space" and commented on the intricacies of "reflections from accidental causes." But he maintained a commitment to local color typical of mid-nineteenth-century American landscape painting, not daring to tamper too much with Creation. His stroke in the *Studies from Nature* is spontaneous and painterly, but it never employs the bright, broken palette of the French Impressionists and Post-Impressionists. Even Courbet used small flecks of color in his trees and rocks. But Durand's experience in the American woods was not the same as Courbet's at Barbizon or Cézanne's in Provence. Durand ate apple pie; Courbet and Cézanne ate *tarte de pomme tartin*. And as Henry James (1843-1916) was to observe, the apple of America had a different taste.

It was with Henry's older brother, William, that Durand had most in common. William James (1842-1910) codified pragmatism into a philosophical system, validating the procedural practice of many American artists that preceded him. "Theories," said James, "become instruments, not answers to enigmas, in which we can rest. We don't lie back on them, we move forward, and on occasion, make nature over again by their aid." A touch of the pragmatic is a constant in the American artist's approach to nature. Durand carried it so far forward that he underscored the notion of the pragmatic as a distinguishing mark of American procedure. It can also be recognized outside the realm of art in areas such as science and invention. For this reason, perhaps, the twentieth-century poet Charles Olson (1910-1970) singled out pragmatism as, "still the conspicuous difference of American from any other

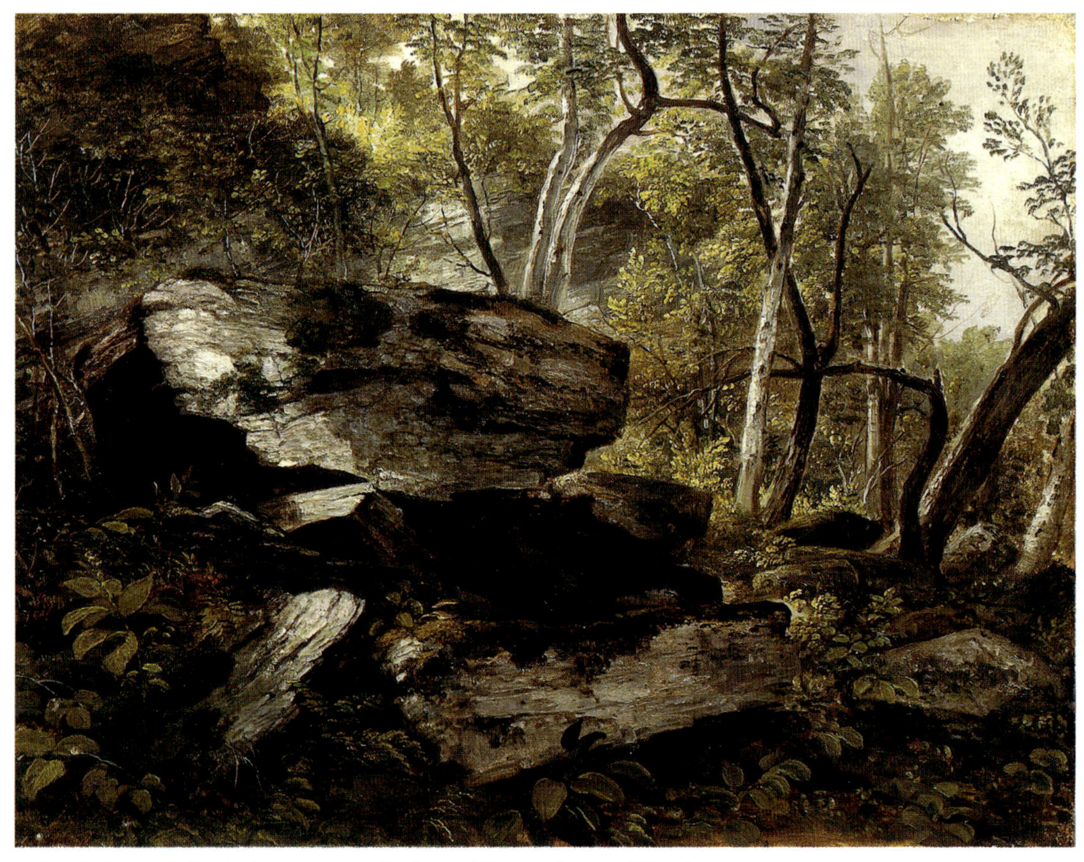

Asher B. Durand, *Study from Nature: Rocks and Trees*, about 1856, oil on canvas.
Gift of Mrs. Lucy Maria Durand Woodman, daughter of the artist, 1907.26

past or any other present, no matter how much we are now almost the true international to which all bow and acknowledge."

But though William James, ever the American, had formulated a philosophy encouraging the pragmatist to "make nature over again" and to "turn towards concreteness," he also acknowledged that the practice of pragmatism did not preclude religion: "The oddly-named thing pragmatism...can remain religious like the rationalisms, but at the same time, like the empiricisms...preserve the richest intimacy with facts." This could be a text for Durand's reconciliation of pragmatic observation with the American tropism towards spirit, through which he joined with Cole and Bryant in their reverence for each twig and branch—the sanctity of nature in which nineteenth-century Americans believed more strongly than their European counterparts. As Irving Howe (1920-1993) once said, in America there are angels in every tree. Was Emerson referring to this union of the pragmatic with the spiritual when he wrote of "the remarkable trait in the American character...the union not very infrequent of Yankee cleverness and spiritualism"?

In his extraordinary nature studies Durand fused two of the major characteristics of American experience in the mid-nineteenth century, empiricism and spirit, faith, belief. In the American woods he captured what Bryant had called "the absence of those tamings and softenings of cultivation...a far-spread wildness, a look as if the new world was fresher from the hand of Him who made it...abstracting the mind from the associations of human agency" and carrying it "up to the idea of a mightier power and to the great mystery of the origin of things." Durand's self-emancipation from convention in the mid-nineteenth century in America made a major contribution to the development of international landscape painting that has still to be acknowledged. The works in this exhibition may accomplish that for him, and for us.

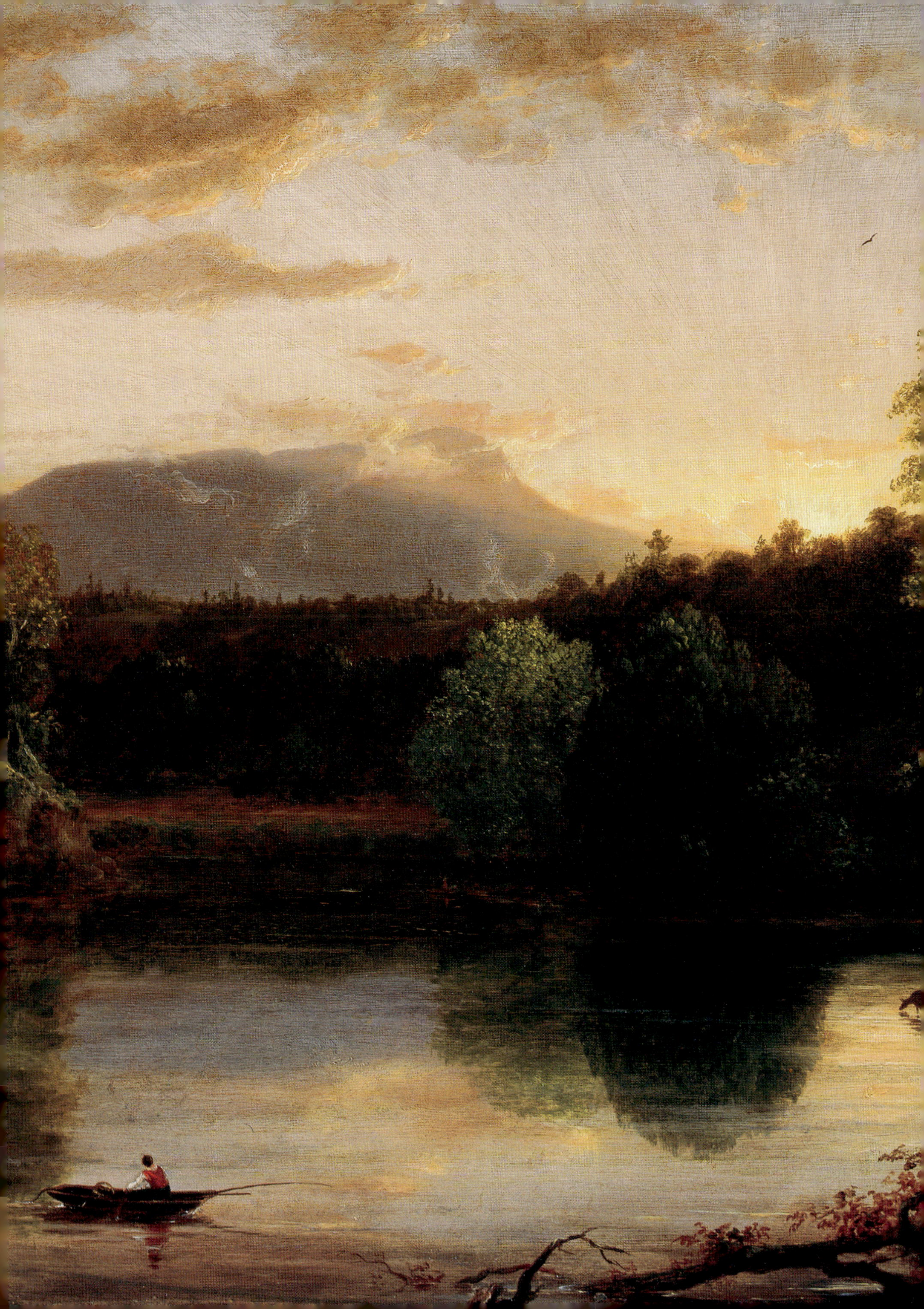

Featured Works

All works are held in the museum and library collections of The New-York Historical Society unless otherwise noted. Dimensions of works of art are given with height preceding width, and in the case of three-dimensional objects, followed by depth.

Thomas Cole (1801-1848)

Italian Scene. Composition, 1833
Oil on canvas
37 1/2 x 54 1/2 inches
Gift of the New-York Gallery of Fine Arts, 1858.19
(illustrated, page 17)

Sunset (View on Catskill Creek, New York), 1833
Oil on wood panel
16 1/2 x 24 1/2 inches, oval
Gift of the New-York Gallery of Fine Arts, 1858.44
(detail illustrated, left)

Moonlight, about 1833-34
Oil on canvas, relined
24 5/8 x 31 3/4 inches
Gift of the New-York Gallery of Fine Arts, 1858.31

Autumn Twilight, View of Corway Peak (Mt. Chocorua), New Hampshire, 1834
Oil on wood panel
13 3/4 x 19 1/2 inches
Gift of the New-York Gallery of Fine Arts, 1858.42

View on Catskill Creek, 1834
Oil on wood panel
13 1/2 x 19 1/2 inches
Gift of the New-York Gallery of Fine Arts, 1858.46

The Course of Empire: The Savage State, not dated
Oil on canvas
39 1/4 x 63 1/4 inches
Gift of the New-York Gallery of Fine Arts, 1858.1
(illustrated, pages 48-49)

The Course of Empire: The Arcadian or Pastoral State, not dated
Oil on canvas
39 1/4 x 63 1/4 inches
Gift of the New-York Gallery of Fine Arts, 1858.2
(illustrated, pages 38-39)

The Course of Empire: The Consummation of Empire, 1835-36
Oil on canvas
51 1/4 x 76 inches
Gift of the New-York Gallery of Fine Arts, 1858.3
(illustrated, pages 20-21)

The Course of Empire: The Consummation of Empire
Inscription on stretcher
Oil on pine board
19 7/8 x 42 1/8 inches
Inv. 4815

Detail, Thomas Cole, *Sunset (View on Catskill Creek, New York)*, 1833, oil on wood panel. Gift of the New-York Gallery of Fine Arts, 1858.44

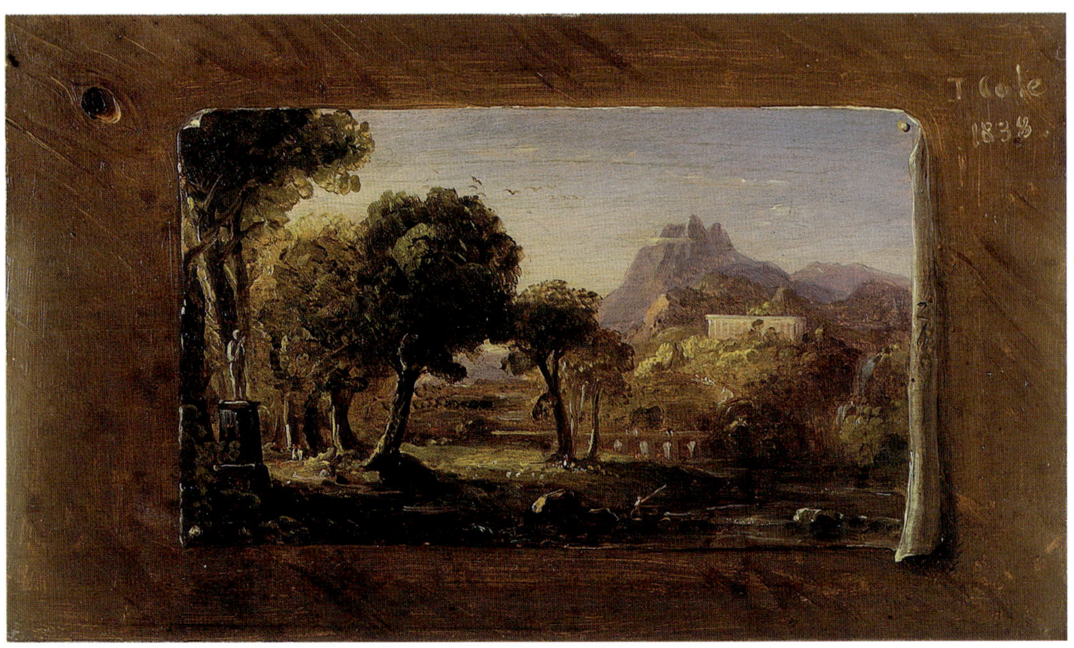

Thomas Cole, *Study for Dream of Arcadia*, 1838, oil on wood panel.
Gift of the children of Asher B. Durand, through John Durand, 1903.9

The Course of Empire: Destruction, 1836
Oil on canvas
39 1/4 x 63 1/2 inches
Gift of the New-York Gallery of Fine Arts, 1858.4
(illustrated, pages 50-51)

The Course of Empire: Desolation, 1836
Oil on canvas
39 1/4 x 63 1/4 inches
Gift of the New-York Gallery of Fine Arts, 1858.5
(illustrated, pages 24-25)

Self-portrait, about 1836
Oil on canvas
22 x 18 inches
Purchase, The Watson Fund, 1964.41
(illustrated, right)

Study for Dream of Arcadia, 1838
Oil on wood panel
8 3/4 x 14 1/2 inches
Gift of the children of Asher B. Durand, through John Durand, 1903.9
(illustrated, above)

The Vale and Temple of Segestae, Sicily, 1844
Oil on canvas
44 1/4 x 66 inches
Gift of the New-York Gallery of Fine Arts, 1858.62

Catskill Creek, New York, 1845
Oil on canvas
26 1/2 x 36 inches
The Robert L. Stuart Collection, on permanent loan from The New York Public Library, Stuart 157

Undated Works

Mountain Scenery
Oil on canvas
22 x 17 inches
The Robert L. Stuart Collection, on permanent loan from The New York Public Library, Stuart 230

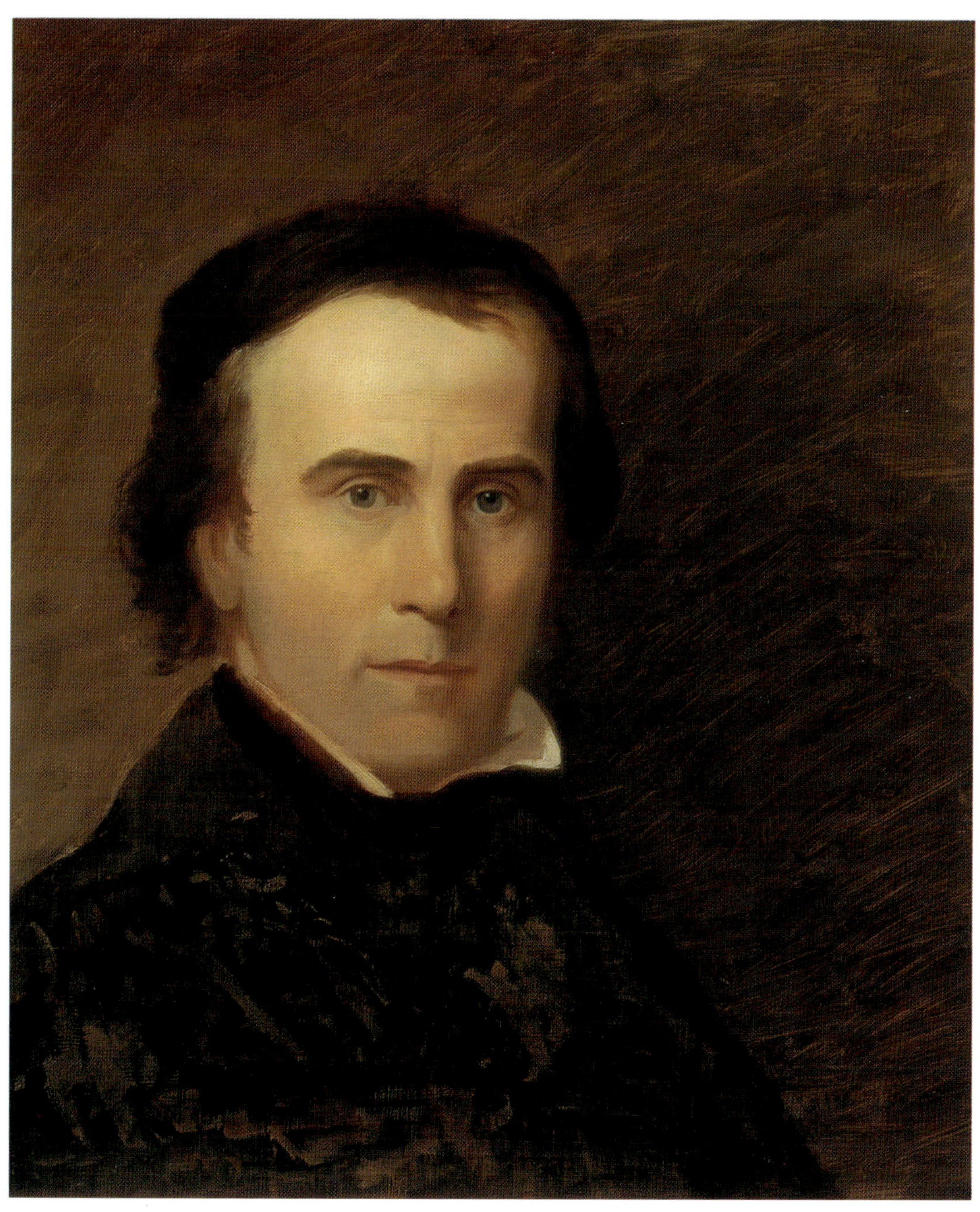

Thomas Cole, *Self-portrait*, about 1836, oil on canvas.
Purchase, The Watson Fund, 1964.41

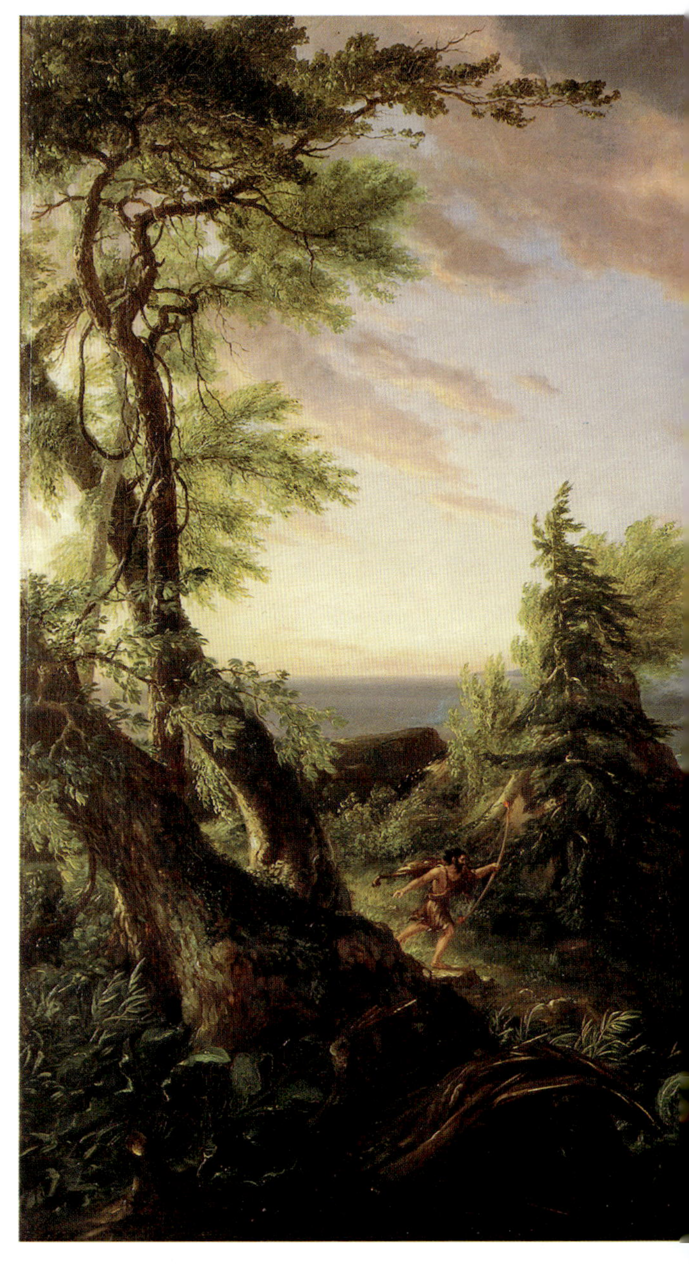

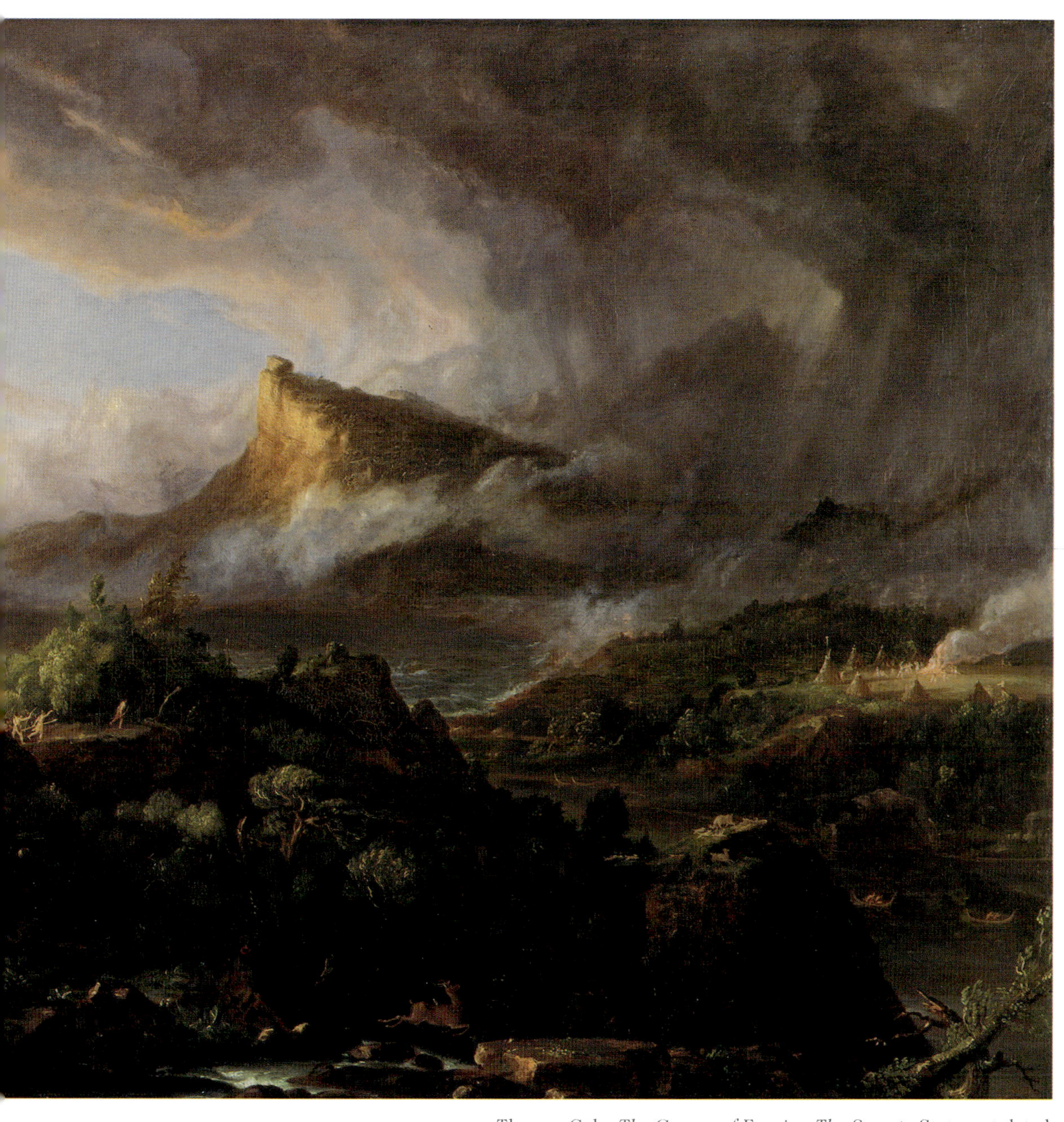

Thomas Cole, *The Course of Empire: The Savage State*, not dated, oil on canvas. Gift of the New-York Gallery of Fine Arts, 1858.1

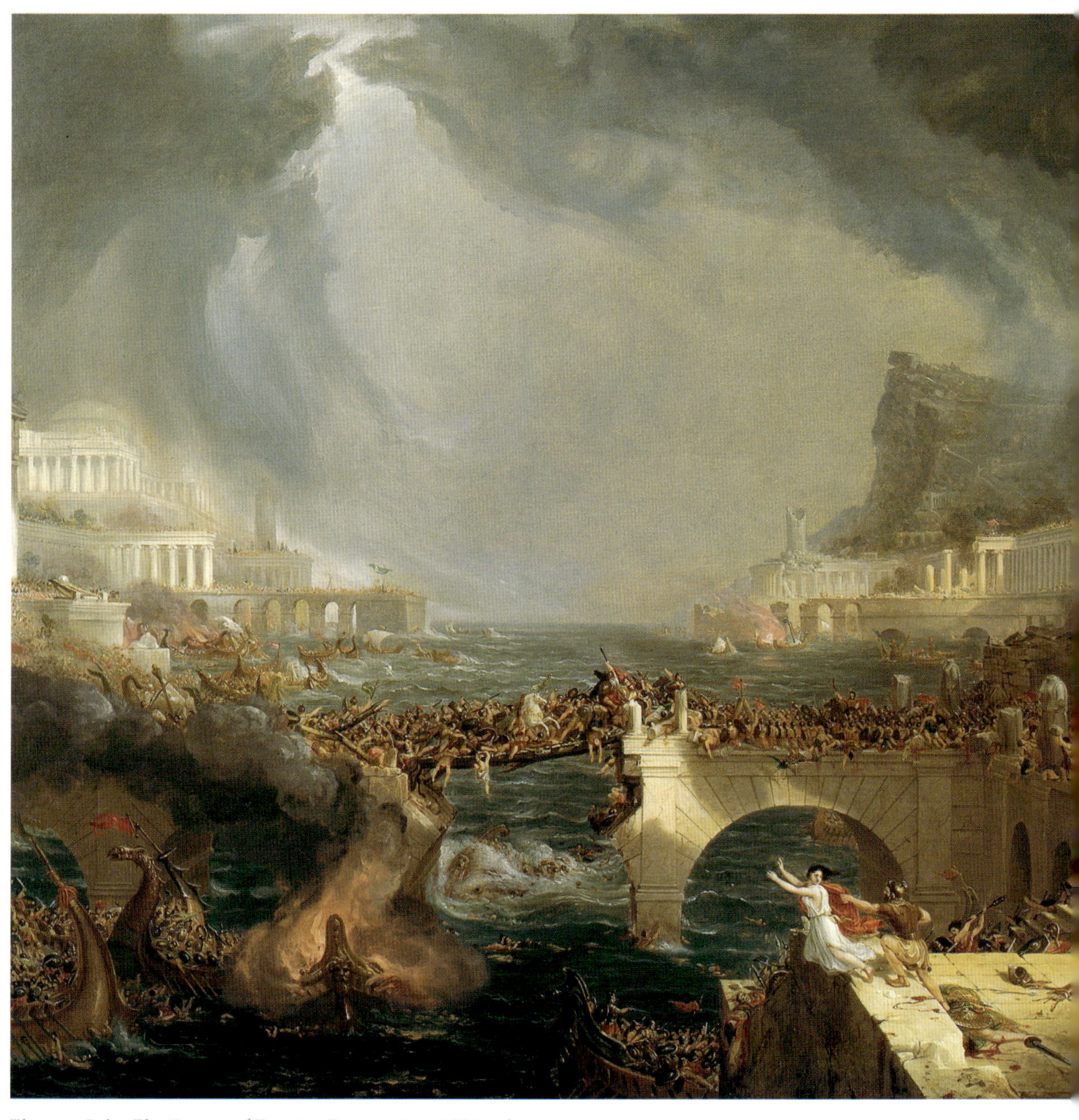

Thomas Cole, *The Course of Empire: Destruction*, 1836, oil on canvas.
Gift of the New-York Gallery of Fine Arts, 1858.4

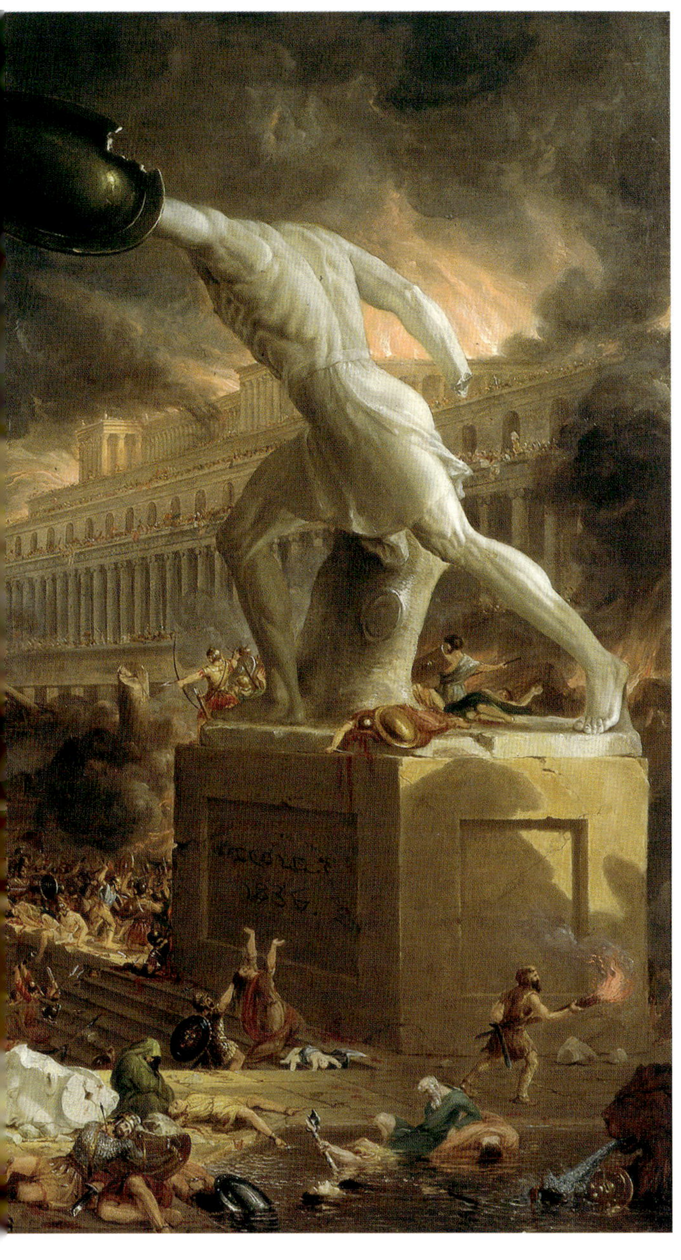

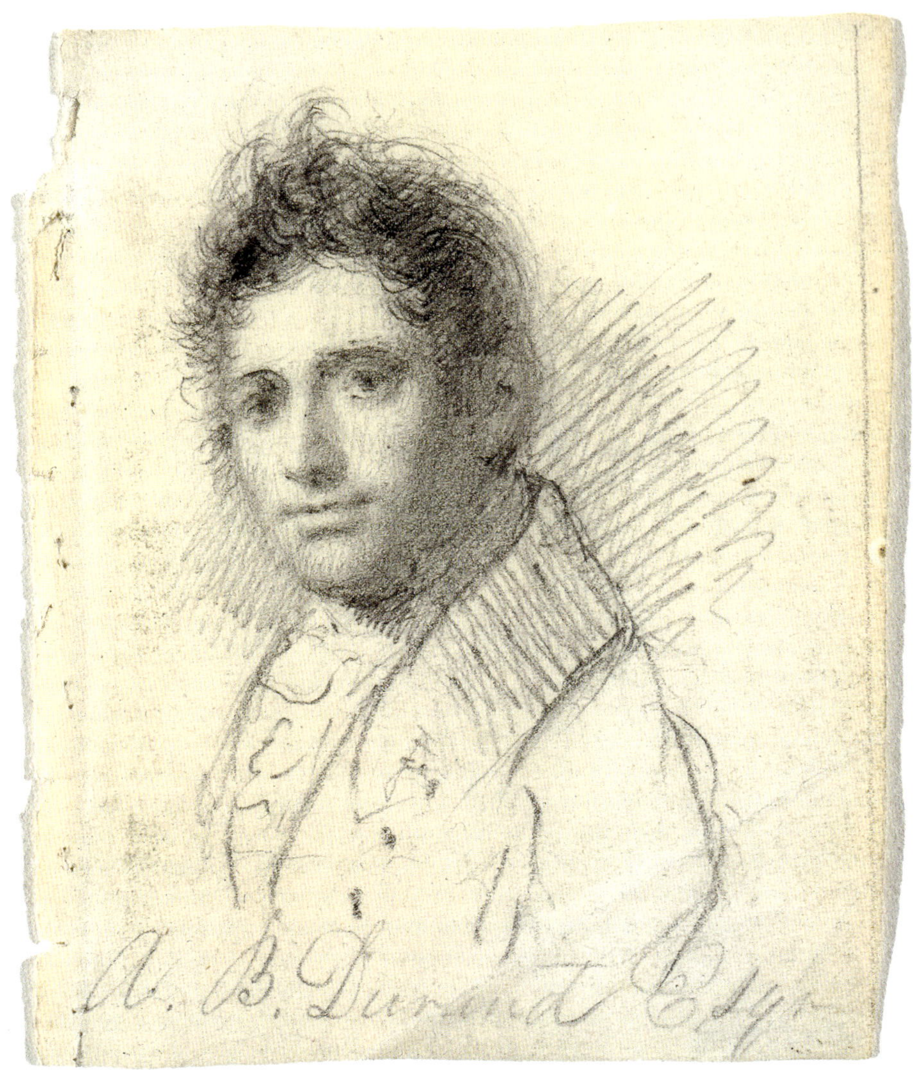

Asher B. Durand, *Self-portrait*, about 1819, pencil on paper. Gift of the Estate of Miss Nora Durand Woodman through Hannah Woodman, 1942.550

Asher B. Durand (1796-1886)

Self-portrait, about 1819
Pencil on paper
3 3/8 x 2 3/4 inches
Gift of the Estate of Miss Nora Durand Woodman through Hannah Woodman, 1942.550
(illustrated, page 52)

Mrs. Asher Brown Durand, 1825
Oil on canvas
24 x 20 inches, oval
Gift of Miss Nora Durand Woodman, granddaughter of the artist, 1918.20

Self-portrait, about 1830-33
Pencil on paper
10 x 7 3/4 inches
Gift of Miss Nora Durand Woodman, granddaughter of the artist 1935.7

Study from Nature, Hoboken, New Jersey, about 1834
Oil on canvas
14 x 10 1/4 inches
Gift of the Children of the Artist, through John Durand, 1903.7

Study from Nature, Hoboken, New Jersey, about 1834
Oil on canvas
11 x 14 1/4 inches
Gift of the Children of the Artist, through John Durand, 1903.8

Luman Reed, 1835
Oil on canvas
30 x 25 inches
Gift of the New-York Gallery of Fine Arts, 1858.56

Sketchbook Fragments, Schroon Lake, New York, 1837
Pencil on paper
9 1/4 x 13 1/4 inches
Gift of Miss Nora Durand Woodman, granddaughter of the artist, 1918.86

Study of Plants, possibly 1837
Pencil on paper
10 1/8 x 6 7/8 inches
Gift of Miss Nora Durand Woodman, granddaughter of the artist, 1918.96

Sketchbook, 1840-41
Pencil and some watercolor on paper
11 1/4 x 17 3/8 inches
Gift of Miss Nora Durand Woodman, granddaughter of the artist, X.486

Sketchbook, 1841
Pencil on paper
9 1/4 x 12 5/8 inches
Gift of Miss Nora Durand Woodman, granddaughter of the artist, 1918.59

Study at Marblestown, Ulster County, New York, about 1845
Oil on canvas
21 3/8 x 16 7/8 inches
Purchase, The Louis Durr Fund, 1887.7

William Cullen Bryant, about 1845
Oil on canvas
30 x 25 inches
Collection of The Century Association, New York, 1879

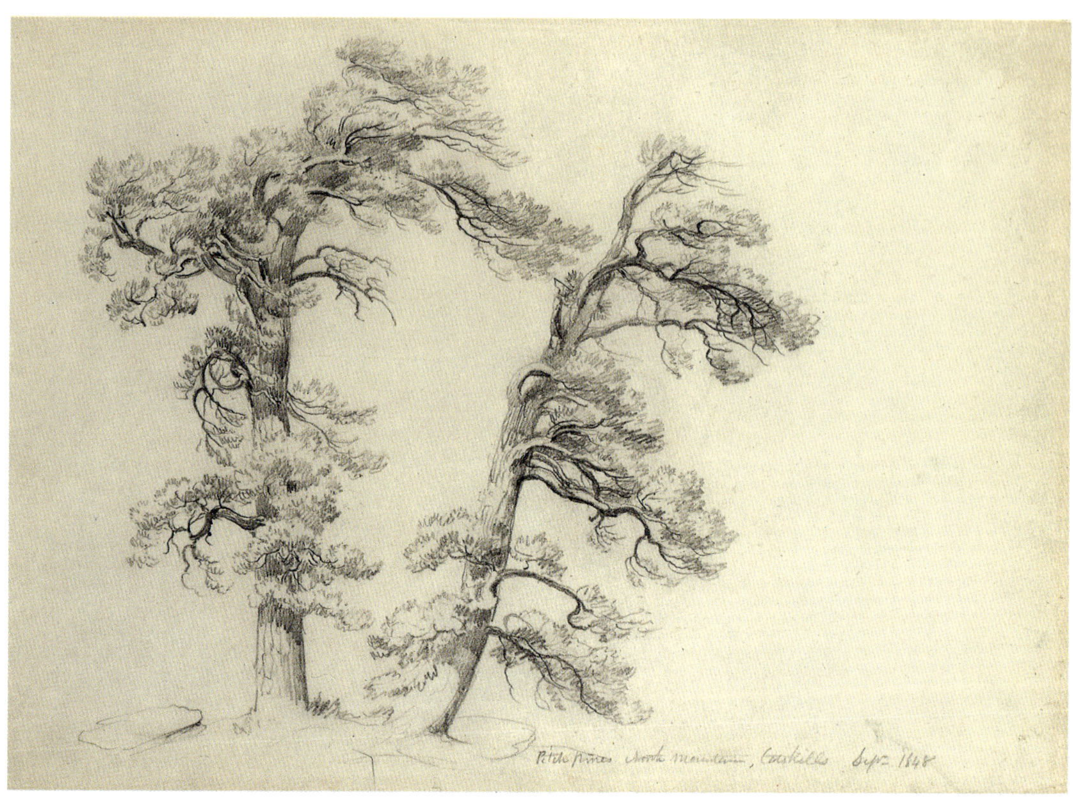

Asher B. Durand, *Study of Trees, Catskill Mountains, New York*, 1848, pencil on paper.
Gift of Miss Nora Durand Woodman, 1918.73

Trees by the Brookside, Kingston, New York, about 1846
Oil on canvas
21 1/4 x 16 3/4 inches
Purchase, The Louis Durr Fund, 1887.6

Buttonwood Trunks, Catskill Clove, New York, 1848
Pencil on paper
13 15/16 x 9 15/16 inches
Gift of Miss Nora Durand Woodman, granddaughter of the artist, 1918.82

Study of Trees, Catskill Mountains, New York, 1848
Pencil on paper
9 15/16 x 13 15/16 inches
Gift of Miss Nora Durand Woodman, granddaughter of the artist, 1918.73
(illustrated, above)

Nature Study, Two Trees, 1851
Oil on canvas
21 x 16 1/2 inches
Gift of Miss Nora Durand Woodman, granddaughter of the artist, 1932.48

Study from Nature, Stratton Notch, Vermont, 1853
Oil on canvas
18 x 23 3/4 inches
Gift of Mrs. Lucy Maria Durand Woodman, daughter of the artist, 1907.21
(illustrated, right and on frontispiece)

Nature Study, 1853
Oil on canvas
16 x 20 inches
Gift of Miss Nora Durand Woodman, granddaughter of the artist, 1932.53

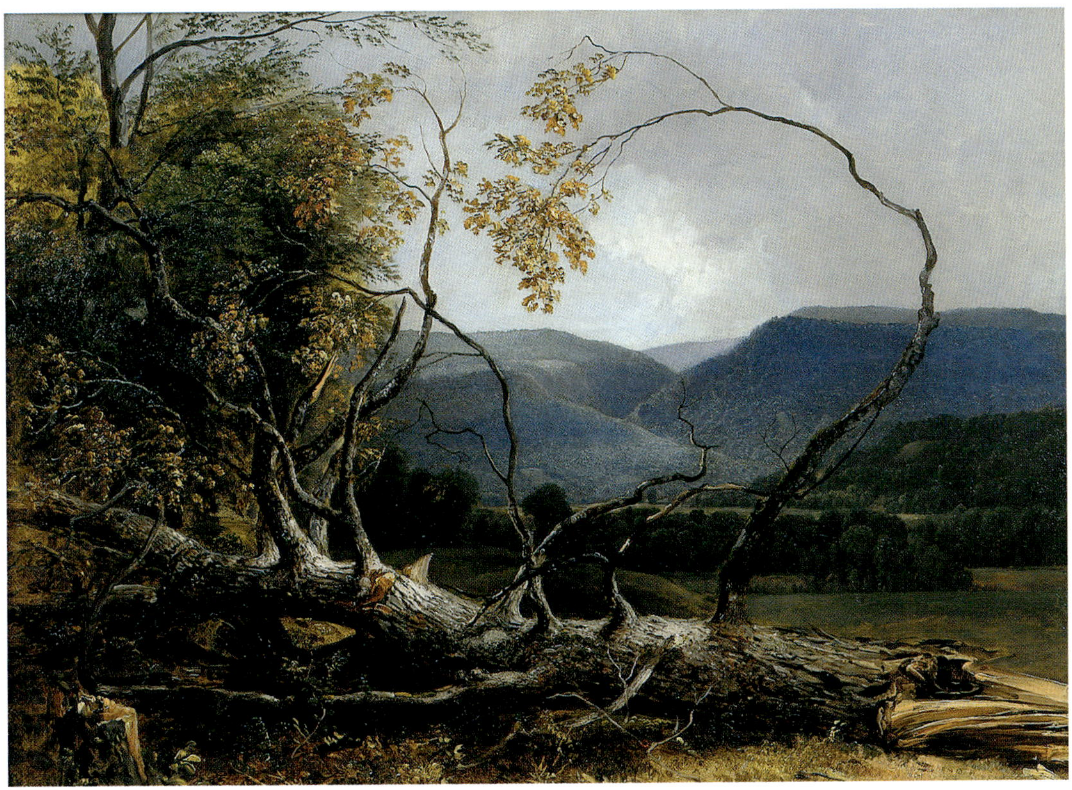

Asher B. Durand, *Study from Nature, Stratton Notch, Vermont*, 1853, oil on canvas. Gift of Mrs. Lucy Maria Durand Woodman, daughter of the artist, 1907.21

Landscape: Trees and Brook, about 1854
Oil on canvas
31 3/4 x 41 inches
Gift of Miss Nora Durand Woodman, granddaughter of the artist, 1930.12

Near Shokan, Ulster County, New York, about 1854
Oil on canvas
16 7/8 x 23 7/8 inches
Gift of Miss Nora Durand Woodman, granddaughter of the artist, 1932.20

Primeval Forest, about 1854
Sepia oil on canvas
58 x 48 inches
Gift of Mrs. Lucy Maria Durand Woodman, daughter of the artist, 1907.18

Group of Trees, about 1855-57
Oil on canvas
24 x 18 inches
Purchase, The Louis Durr Fund, 1887.8

Study from Nature, Bronxville, New York, 1856
Oil on canvas
16 3/4 x 24 inches
Gift of Miss Nora Durand Woodman, granddaughter of the artist, 1932.34

Study from Nature: Rocks and Trees, about 1856
Oil on canvas
17 x 21 1/2 inches
Gift of Mrs. Lucy Maria Durand Woodman, daughter of the artist, 1907.26
(illustrated, page 42)

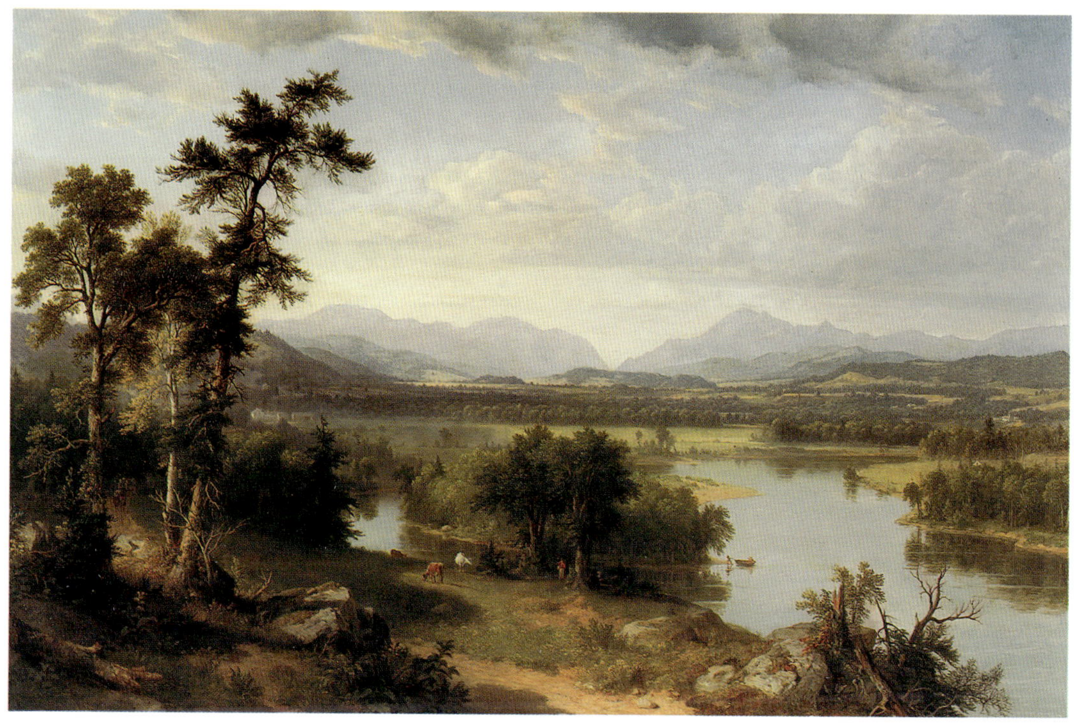

Asher B. Durand, *White Mountain Scenery, Franconia Notch, New Hampshire*, 1857, oil on canvas. The Robert L. Stuart Collection, on permanent loan from the New York Public Library, Stuart 105

Study from Nature: Rocks and Trees in the Catskills, New York, about 1856
Oil on canvas
21 1/2 x 17 inches
Gift of Mrs. Lucy Maria Durand Woodman, daughter of the artist, 1907.20

Study of a Fallen Tree Trunk, Catskill Mountains, New York, 1857
Pencil on paper
9 13/16 x 14 1/2 inches
Gift of Miss Nora Durand Woodman, granddaughter of the artist, 1918.149

White Mountain Scenery, Franconia Notch, New Hampshire, 1857
Oil on canvas
48 1/4 x 72 1/2 inches
The Robert L. Stuart Collection, on permanent loan from the New York Public Library, Stuart 105
(illustrated, above; detail on cover)

Study of the Branch Structure of a Tree, Geneseo, New York, 1859
Pencil heightened with white on paper
14 x 10 inches
Gift of Miss Nora Durand Woodman, granddaughter of the artist, 1918.156

Study of the Branch Structure of a Dead Tree, Fishkill Landing, New York, 1860
Pencil on paper
18 11/16 x 12 1/4 inches
Gift of Miss Nora Durand Woodman, granddaughter of the artist, 1918.61

Study of Branches, Hague, Lake George, New York, about 1862
Pencil heightened with white on paper
12 3/16 x 18 11/16 inches
Gift of Miss Nora Durand Woodman, granddaughter of the artist, 1918.172

Rocks and Brook, Bolton, Lake George, New York, 1863
Pencil on paper
12 5/16 x 18 1/2 inches
Gift of Miss Nora Durand Woodman, granddaughter of the artist, 1918.177

Study of Rocks, Bolton, Lake George, New York, about 1863
Pencil heightened with white on paper
12 3/16 x 18 5/8 inches
Gift of Miss Nora Durand Woodman, granddaughter of the artist, 1918.71

Study of Rocks with Sketch of Trees, Bolton, Lake George, New York, about 1863
Pencil heightened with white on paper
12 3/16 x 18 5/8 inches
Gift of Miss Nora Durand Woodman, granddaughter of the artist, 1918.187

Catskill Clove, New York, 1864
Oil on canvas
15 1/8 x 24 inches
Gift of Miss Nora Durand Woodman, granddaughter of the artist, 1932.14

Two Studies of Trees, Santa Cruz Road, Catskill Clove, New York, 1865
Pencil on paper
12 1/4 x 19 9/16 inches
Gift of Miss Nora Durand Woodman, granddaughter of the artist, 1918.81

Sketchbook, 1867-70
Pencil on paper
4 1/2 x 7 3/4 inches
X.487

Catskill Study, New York, about 1870
Oil on canvas
17 x 24 inches
Gift of Miss Nora Durand Woodman, granddaughter of the artist, 1932.13

Black Mountain from the Harbor Islands, Lake George, New York, about 1874
Pencil heightened with white on paper
9 7/8 x 18 7/8 inches
Gift of Miss Nora Durand Woodman, granddaughter of the artist, 1935.9

Undated Works

Lower Part of Four Tree Trunks
Pencil on paper
12 1/2 x 9 5/8 inches
Gift of Miss Nora Durand Woodman, granddaughter of the artist, 1918.325
(illustrated, page 61)

Rocks
Pencil heightened with white on paper
12 1/8 x 18 5/8 inches
Gift of Miss Nora Durand Woodman, granddaughter of the artist, 1918.333

Sketchbook #3
Graphite heightened with white
9 1/4 x 12 1/4 inches
Gift of Miss Nora Durand Woodman, granddaughter of the artist, 1918.60

Study of the Branch Structure of a Tree, Scarsdale
Pencil on paper
12 1/4 x 18 5/8 inches
Gift of Miss Nora Durand Woodman, granddaughter of the artist, 1918.257

Study of Rocks, Hoboken, New Jersey
Pencil heightened with white on paper
9 7/8 x 13 1/8 inches
Gift of Miss Nora Durand Woodman, granddaughter of the artist, 1918.249

Study of Trees, Shandaken, New York
Pencil on paper
14 x 10 inches
Gift of Miss Nora Durand Woodman, granddaughter of the artist, 1918.260
(illustrated, page 28)

Study of Trees by a Brook, Scarsdale
Pencil on paper
12 1/16 x 18 5/8 inches
Gift of Miss Nora Durand Woodman, granddaughter of the artist, 1918.259

Two Trees without Foliage
Pencil on paper
13 3/4 x 19 15/16 inches
Gift of Miss Nora Durand Woodman, granddaughter of the artist, 1918.304

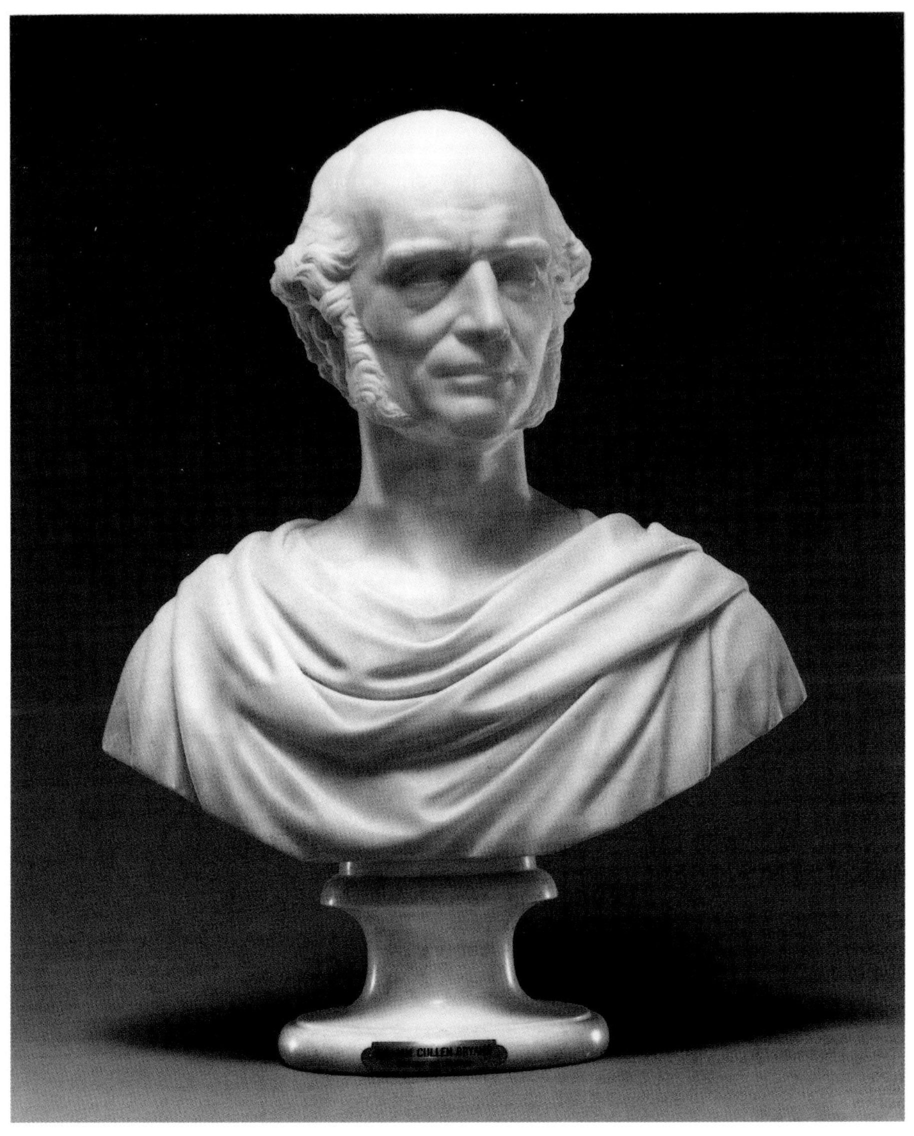

Henry Kirke Brown (1814-1886), *William Cullen Bryant*, 1846, marble.
Bequest of Charles M. Leupp, 1860.6

William Cullen Bryant (1794-1878)

Poems
(Cambridge, Mass.: Hillard and Metcalf, 1821)

[with Asher B. Durand (1796-1886)]
American Landscape
(New York: Elam Bliss, 1830)

Editorials on Slavery and The Park
New York Evening Post, July 31, 1844

A Funeral Oration, occasioned by the death of Thomas Cole, delivered before the National Academy of Design, New York, May 4, 1848
(New York: D. Appleton & Co., 1848)
Collection of the National Academy Museum

Letter to Richard Parker
May 21, 1849
William Cullen Bryant Papers

The Home Book of the Picturesque: Home Authors and Home Artists; or, American Scenery, Art and Literature
(New York: G. P. Putnam, 1852)

"The Garden of Alcinous, from the Seventh Book of Homer's *Odyssey*"
September 11, 1865
Miscellaneous Manuscripts, Bryant, William Cullen

Letter to John Rogers
October 18, 1869

"Mental Photograph by the Subject"
New York, March 1870
Collection of The Century Association Archives Foundation, New York

Among the Trees
(New York: G. P. Putnam, 1874)

Bryant's First and Last Poems: I. Thanatopsis, II. The Flood of Years
(New York: G. P. Putnam, 1878-79)

Undated Works

"A Mighty Realm is the Land of Dreams"
Miscellaneous Manuscripts, Bryant, William Cullen
(illustrated, page 62)

Miscellaneous Works

John Trumbull (1756-1843)
Asher B. Durand, 1826
Oil on wood panel
25 1/4 x 20 3/4 inches
Purchase, The Louis Durr Fund, 1895.13

Henry Inman (1801-1846)
William Cullen Bryant, 1827
Watercolor and pencil on paper
4 1/2 x 4 inches
Gift of Anna R. Fairchild, 1910.20

Minutes of The Sketch Club
1 vol. (January-December, 1829)
The Century Association Archives Foundation, New York

Minutes of The Sketch Club
2 vols. (December 1830-April 1833)
The Century Association Archives Foundation, New York

G. C. Verplanck (1786-1870), W. C. Bryant (1794-1878) and Robert C. Sands (1799-1832)
Miscellanies, First Published Under the Name of the Talisman, Volume III
(New York: Elam Bliss, 1833)

Daniel Huntington (1816-1906)
Thomas Cole, 1841
Oil on canvas
29 3/4 x 24 3/4 inches
Purchase, The Louis Durr Fund, 1939.161

Louis L. Noble (1813-1882)
Letter to William Cullen Bryant
March 20, 1848
New York Public Library, Manuscript Division, Bryant-Godwin Papers

Henry Peters Gray (1819-1877)
William Cullen Bryant, 1850
Oil on canvas
30 1/2 x 25 1/4 inches
Gift of The American Art-Union, 1863.5

Louis L. Noble (1813-1882)
Letter to William Cullen Bryant
November 18, 1851
New York Public Library, Manuscript Division, Bryant-Godwin Papers

Louis L. Noble (1813-1882)
The Course of Empire, Voyage of Life, and Other Pictures of Thomas Cole with Selections from his Letters and Miscellaneous Writings
(New York: Cornish Lamport & Co., 1853)

The Crayon
Vol. 1 (January-June, 1855)

Louis L. Noble (1812-1882)
After Icebergs with a Painter: Summer Voyage to Labrador and Around New Foundland
(London: Sampson Low, 1861)

Charles Sumner (1811-1874)
Letter to William Cullen Bryant
Boston, October 5, 1863
New York Public Library, Manuscript Division, Bryant-Godwin Papers

Launt Thompson (1833-1894)
William Cullen Bryant, about 1865
Marble bust
21 x 13 x 12 inches
Collection of The Century Association, New York, 1892

Napoleon Sarony (1821-1896)
William Cullen Bryant, 1868
Albumen silver print
10 x 8 inches
Collection of The Century Association, New York, 1874

Tiffany & Co.
Presentation Vase, 1875-76
Silver
33 1/2 x 14 x 11 5/16 inches
Collection of The Metropolitan Museum of Art, Gift of William Cullen Bryant, 1877
(illustrated, page 8)

"[Obituary] William Cullen Bryant"
The Daily Graphic
Wednesday, June 12, 1878

John Rogers (1829-1904)
William Cullen Bryant, 1892
Plaster bust
24 1/4 x 20 x 13 3/4 inches
Gift of Miss Katherine Rebecca Rogers, daughter of the artist, 1936.712

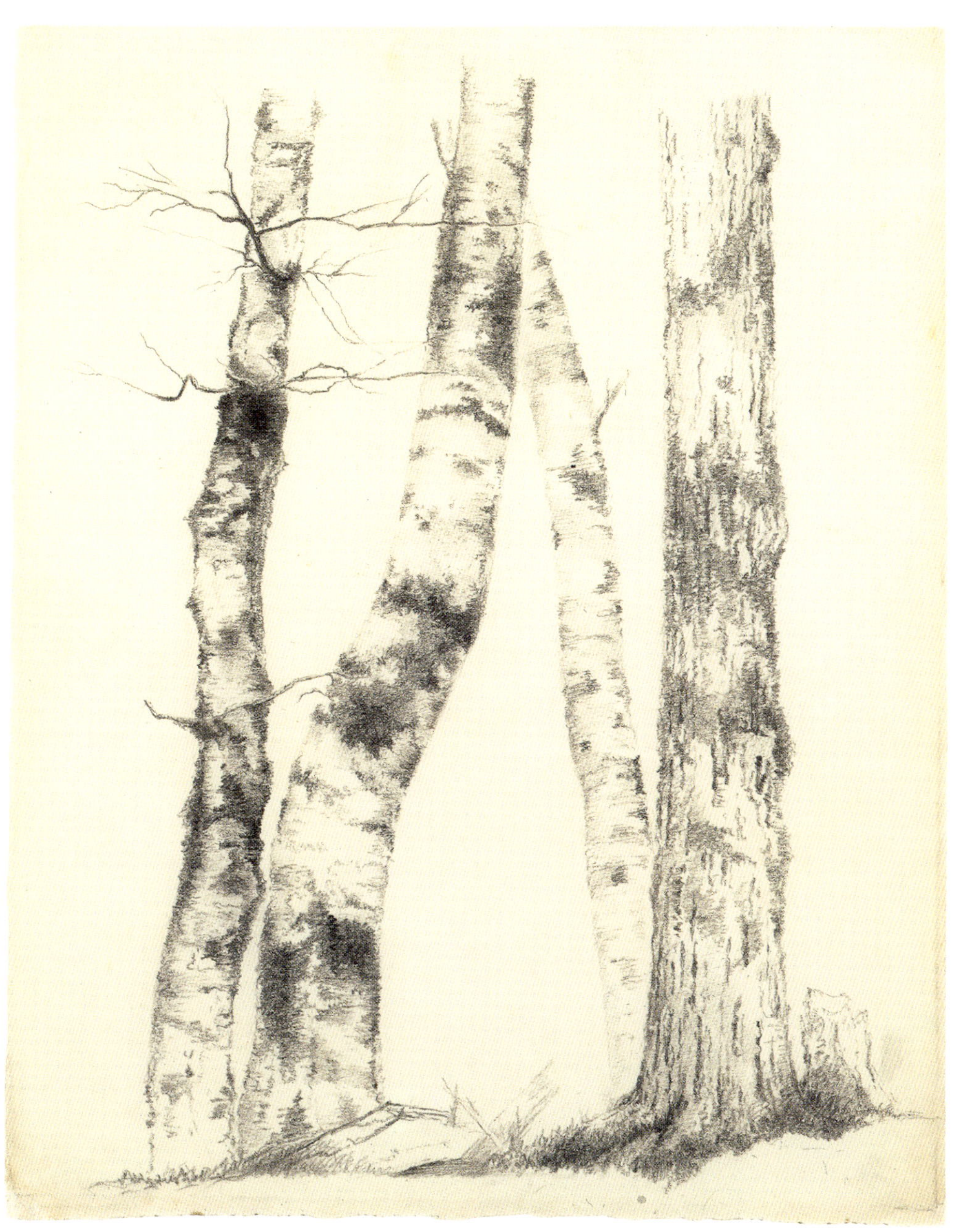

Asher B. Durand, *Lower Part of Four Tree Trunks,* not dated, pencil on paper.
Gift of Miss Nora Durand Woodman, granddaughter of the artist, 1918.325

A mighty realm is the Land of Dreams
With steeps that hang in the twilight sky
And weltering oceans and trailing streams
That gleam where the dusky valleys lie.

But over its shadowy border flow
Sweet ~~beams~~ rays from the world of endless morn
And the nearer mountains catch the glow
And flowers in the nearer fields are born

The souls of the happy dead repair
From their bowers of light to that bordering land
And walk in the fainter glory there
With the souls of the living hand in hand.

One calm sweet smile in that shadowy sphere
From eyes that open on earth no more
One warning word from a voice once dear
How they rise in the memory oer and oer.

Far off from those hills that shine with day
And fields that bloom in the heavenly gales,
The Land of Dreams goes stretching away
To dimmer mountains and darker vales.

There lie the chambers of guilty delight
There walk the spectres of guilty fear
And soft low voices that float through the night
Are whispering sin in the helpless ear.

William Cullen Bryant, "A Mighty Realm is the Land of Dreams"
Miscellaneous Manuscripts, Bryant, William Cullen"2

Selected Bibliography

Boylan, James, "William Cullen Bryant," in *American Newspaper Journalists, 1690-1872*, Perry J. Ashley, ed. (Detroit: Gale Research Company, 1985), 43.

Bradley, William Aspenwall, *William Cullen Bryant* (New York: The Macmillan Company, 1905).

Bryant, William Cullen, *The American Landscape* (New York: Elam Bliss, 1830).

Bryant, William Cullen, *A Funeral Oration, Occasioned by the Death of Thomas Cole, Delivered Before the National Academy of Design, New-York, May 4, 1848* (New York: D. Appleton & Co., 1848).

Bryant, William Cullen, *The Home Book of the Picturesque: Home Authors and Home Artists; or, American Scenery, Art and Literature* (New York: G. P. Putnam, 1852).

Bryant, William Cullen, *Letter of a Traveler; or, Notes of Things Seen in Europe and America* (New York: G. P. Putnam, 1852).

Bryant, William Cullen, Miscellaneous Manuscripts.

Bryant, William Cullen, "Mental Photograph by the Subject," The Century Association, New York.

Bryant, William Cullen, *Miscellanies: First Published under the Name of the Talisman* (New York: Elam Bliss, 1833).

Bryant, William Cullen, *The Poetical Works of William Cullen Bryant* (New York: D. Appleton & Co., 1929).

Bryant, William Cullen, Scrapbook, The Century Association, New York.

Bryant-Godwin Papers, New York Public Library, New York.

Callow, James T., *Kindred Spirits: Knickerbocker Writers and American Artists, 1807-1855* (Chapel Hill: University of North Carolina Press, 1967).

Dunlap, William, *The History of the Rise and Progress of the Arts of Design in the United States* (New York: Dover Publications, Inc., 1969).

Durand, A. B., "Letters on Landscape Painting," *The Crayon* 1 (January-June 1855): 1-2, 34-35, 66-67, 97-98, 145-46, 209-21, 273-75, 354-55.

Durand, John, *The Life and Times of A. B. Durand* (New York: Da Capo Press, 1970).

Godwin, Parke, *A Biography of William Cullen Bryant with Extracts from His Private Correspondence* (New York: D. Appleton & Co., 1883).

Harrington, K., "William Cullen Bryant," in *American Travel Writers*, Donald Ross and James J. Schramer, eds. (Washington, D.C.: Gale Research, 1987), 189: 49-54.

Homer, *The Odyssey of Homer* (New York: Houghton Mifflin Company, 1871).

Koke, Richard J., *American Landscape and Genre Paintings in the New-York Historical Society* (New York: New-York Historical Society, 1982).

Lawall, David Barnard, *Asher Brown Durand: His Art and Theory in Relation to His Times* (New York: Garland Publishing, Inc., 1977).

McDermott, John J., ed., *The Writings of William James* (Chicago: University of Chicago Press, 1977).

Minutes of the Sketch Club, 1829, The Century Association, New York.

Minutes of the Sketch Club, 1833, The Century Association, New York.

Minutes of the Sketch Club, 1844-69, The Century Association, New York.

Noble, Louis Legrand, *The Life and Works of Thomas Cole* (Cambridge, Mass.: Belknap Press, 1964).

Novak, Barbara, *The Arcadian Landscape: American Painters in Italy* (Kansas City, Kans.: University of Kansas Museum of Art, 1972).

Novak, Barbara, *American Painting of the Nineteenth Century: Realism, Idealism and the American Experience* (New York: Harper & Row, 1979).

Novak, Barbara, *Nature and Culture: American Landscape and Painting 1825-1875* (New York: Oxford University Press, 1980).

Parry, Ellwood C., *The Art of Thomas Cole: Ambition and Imagination* (Newark: University of Delaware Press, 1988).

Pearce, Roy Harvey, *The Continuity of American Poetry* (Princeton, N.J.: Princeton University Press, 1961).

Pinto, Holly Joan, *William Cullen Bryant and the Hudson River School of Landscape Painting* (Roslyn, N.Y.: Nassau County Museum of Fine Art, 1981).

Porte, Joel, ed., *Emerson in His Journals* (Cambridge, Mass.; Harvard University, Belknap Press, 1982).

Tuckerman, Henry Theodore, *Book of the Artists: American Artist Life: Comprising Biographical and Critical Sketches of American Artists: Preceded by an historical account of the rise and progress of art in America* (New York: G. P. Putnam & Sons, 1867).

Tymn, Marshall B., *Thomas Cole's Poetry* (York, Penn.: Liberty Cap Books, 1972).

Wilson, James Grant, *Bryant and his Friends: Some Reminiscences of Knickerbocker Writers* (New York: Ford Howard & Hulbert, 1886).